ZEN AND CREATIVE MANAGEMENT

Albert Low was born in England and holds a degree in philosophy and psychology. He was a business executive up until 1976, when he devoted himself full time to the practice of Zen Buddhism. He studied under Roshi Philip Kapleau and completed his training in 1986, at that time receiving full transmission as a teacher of Zen. Mr. Low is currently the director of the Montreal Zen Centre, and the author of *An Invitation to Practice Zen* and *The Iron Cow of Zen,* both published by Tuttle.

ALBERT LOW

ZEN and CREATIVE MANAGEMENT

CHARLES E. TUTTLE COMPANY
Rutland, Vermont & Tokyo, Japan

Published by the Charles E. Tuttle Company, Inc.
of Rutland, Vermont & Tokyo, Japan
with editorial offices at
2-6 Suido 1-chome, Bunkyo-ku, Tokyo 112
by arrangement with the author

© 1976 by Albert Low

First Tuttle edition, 1992
Second printing, 1993

LCC Card No. 92-60520
ISBN 0-8048-1883-5
Printed in Japan

Dedicated to the
Memory of My Parents

ACKNOWLEDGMENTS

I should like to acknowledge the help that I received from the following people:

Philip Kapleau, Roshi who has patiently guided me over the past number of years in the practice of Zen and who has given constant encouragement and advice in the writing of this book.

The book started with an insight that occurred some years ago when my understanding of the work of Dr. Elliott Jaques and the late Mr. J. G. Bennett coalesced into one whole. My indebtedness to these two writers is very great.

My wife, Jean, helped in the development of the ideas, and has given valuable help in the overall construction of the book through expert and sometimes courageous editing. She has also patiently typed the manuscript more times than I can count.

Mr. D. J. Moore also helped in the development of these ideas through many discussions that we had together. He handled expertly the early administrative work involved in writing the book.

I am also in debt to Barry Nevitt, Bob Campbell, and Saul Kuchinsky, who read the manuscript and made valuable suggestions; to Bob Grant, Kay Grant, and Maurice Hecht, who gave much needed moral support, and to Grace Campbell and Moyna Jarrett who have hunted down innumerable references.

CONTENTS

CONTENTS

Modern capitalism is absolutely irreligious
without internal union, without much public
spirit, often, though not always, a mere
congeries of possessors and pursuers.

Maynard Keynes

Are we confronted with a tragic, insolvable
dilemma? Must we produce a sick people in
order to have a healthy economy, or can we
use our material resources, our inventions,
our computers to serve the ends of man? Must
individuals be passive and dependent in
order to have strong and well-functioning
organizations?

Erich Fromm

"I look at Zen not as a religion but as a way of thinking, and at scientific breakthrough—the joy of creating something—as a form of enlightenment."[1]

"Conflict is the very source of creation; thus, what is most to be feared by the company that wants its management to remain creative, is loss of a sense of conflict through the resolution of conflict by an old man's methods."[2]

Management calls for creativity and reasoning, intuition no less than analysis. The manager does not simply struggle with problems but has to wrestle with dilemmas as well. Dilemmas arise out of the whole; problems come with the luxury of being able to reduce the whole to component parts. With dilemmas, unlike problems, there are no right solutions; one can only choose the most suitable decision. This has always been the case but nowadays managers do not simply have to wrestle with dilemmas that arise within their own companies, but also with those that arise from the interaction of their companies with society as a whole.

Karl Marx said that every system carries within it the seeds of its own destruction. Another way of putting this is to say that when a system comes to maturity, dilemmas rise to the surface. Pollution is fast becoming the number-one threat to the future, outpacing other threats such as overpopulation, depleted resources, and nuclear disasters. Pollution, however, is but one horn of the societal dilemma. The need for full employment is another. The present specters of depression, unemployment, poverty, and disillusionment are the other side of the story. The pendulum will swing again, jobs will once more become plentiful, but how much more litter, discarded chemicals, waste material, and waste gases can our planet survive?

A full dilemma, moreover, as this book will show, has four horns, not just two. The societal dilemma also includes the need to control inflation, which still threatens the financial structure, and also free access to credit, which has become a principle feature of that structure. Each of these four is dependent on the others and none can be resolved in isolation. Each is a dimension of the whole.

Traditional scientific thought has brought us the marvels of the computer, TV, car, airplane, high-rise buildings, air conditioning, labor-saving devices, miracles in medicine, and space exploration. But it is bringing disaster along with it. The very success of scientific medicine has already caused overpopulation: cities are crowded, and we are beginning to fight over scarce resources such as fish, fresh water, and oil. Technology applied to agriculture, through fertilizers and the chemical control of pests, promised to feed the starving millions, but at the cost of soil erosion, air and water pollution. New construction technology has enabled us to produce high-rise buildings, roads, bridges, and airfields; it has also given us urban blight and decay, turned rich land into concrete deserts, and made peace and quiet scarce resources. And this is without an industrially developed Third World.

This is not news. It is something we have worried about and would now prefer to forget. The optimists still look to technology to dig us out of the hole into which we are sliding, a hole which technological thinking dug in the first place. The pessimists are burrowing into computer games, TV sitcoms, and state lotteries, hoping some windfall will save them and their families. Both optimism and pessimism, however, are inappropriate since both rely upon one-sided views of the situation. Even so, both are right! The optimist is right because life will always find a way; the pessimist is right because technology cannot be that way.

Technology is the result of abstraction. Science alters the world in order to be able to cope with it. What can be measured or weighed is accepted, and what cannot is ignored or denied. Technology would fit nature, including the human being, to the procrustean bed of logic and so destroy the organic wholeness that gives life meaning. When this organic wholeness is destroyed, there are parts which no longer fit, or fit badly. For example, instead of wastes being the very basis for new life and growth, they lie on one side—unusable, polluting. When people no longer fit the system, they are unemployed, poor, discarded. In nature there is interpenetration; each is a whole supporting and sustaining the whole. In technology there are only parts; everything is a part of something and everything is ultimately replaceable, and, ultimately, meaningless.

It is not that technology is "bad." It simply lacks any self-regulating mechanism. Technological thinking is a marvelous creation but, as Martin Heidegger has pointed out, it is its very success that must be feared because it so captivates, bewitches, dazzles, and beguiles us that it threatens to become someday accepted and practiced as the only way of thinking. "Then man would have denied and thrown away his special nature—that he is a meditative being . . . The issue is keeping meditative thinking alive."[3]

This meditative, intuitive thinking assumes wholes are intrinsic, that they are relative, and that we cannot reduce the complexity of a whole without changing its nature. This calls for an awareness of the organic integrity of a concrete situation—an openness to all its aspects. In Zen Buddhism such an openness and awareness is called Zazen. Within the practice of Zen lies an alternative way, one of the very few remaining ways, of facing our predicament.

Zen is the outcome of the profound need each of us has for meaning, which can only truly be found when we have understood clearly who and what we are. Zen is not exotic or otherworldly; it concerns practice more than theory. In the practice of Zen a person comes to terms with life in a meaningful way. Many would say that if only they could become better managers, their lives would be more meaningful. It would be truer to say that if we could find our true meaning, we would stand a chance of becoming better managers. Becoming a better manager would be a byproduct of a practice aimed at reaching the source of our most pressing need: the need to be whole and significant. The solutions to our managerial problems are inextricably connected to the solutions to our personal problems.

This book has taken shape over several years and is offered with several aims in mind. First, it is hoped that some of what is suggested will strike a resonant chord in the minds of readers and give them direction for their own consideration of organizational issues. The book also attempts to show the value of applying another way of thinking to life situations, a value that far exceeds what can be derived from simply solving organizational problems. Lastly, it is hoped that the ideas developed here will illustrate the compatibility of organizations and this way of thinking.

The life force that organizes species, organs, and organisms also molds organizations. Human beings cannot conquer nature—they are nature in action. The creative leaps made by man and the creative leaps made by nature are of the same kind. Nature makes use of what may be called *"un reculer pour mieux sauter,"* [4] a recoiling, in order to leap that much better. When nature's evolutionary drive has reached a cul-de-sac, it withdraws and breaks out from a new point in a new direction. I am suggesting that Zazen is a discipline that uses *un reculer pour mieux sauter;* this approach provides greater facility in dealing with those organizational cul-de-sacs that are both frustrations and opportunities. Zazen seems to be as old as mankind; what is new today is its availability to the West, and specifically, its availability for dealing with the complex, multifaceted problems encountered in organizations.[5]

ZEN AND CREATIVE MANAGEMENT

1. SHAREHOLDER, EMPLOYEE, CUSTOMER: THE BASIC TRIAD

A company is a multidimensional system capable of growth, expansion, and self-regulation. It is, therefore, not a thing, but a set of interacting forces. Any theory of organization must be capable of reflecting a company's many facets, its dynamism, and its basic orderliness. When a company organization is reviewed, or when reorganizing a company, it must be looked upon as a whole, as a total system.

A system can be defined as a set of independent but mutually related elements.[1] The different jobs or functions in a company are the "independent elements"; each has its own reason for being; each is done by a different manager, each of whom is expected to act to some extent as an autonomous and independent whole. This, after all, is what we mean by responsibility. *But the mutual relatedness of the job with other jobs in the company is as important a feature of the organization as the content of the job itself.*

This mutual relationship corresponds to the structure of the whole, and it must be emphasized because it is frequently ignored when organizations are reviewed. When managers reorganize they often do not give very much attention to how parts of the system are related in time or structure. Furthermore, this relatedness is something that is poorly understood. For example, managers frequently write job descriptions in complete isolation from other job descriptions and even in isolation from what the company as a whole is trying to do. Although organization charts are drawn, they often ignore the content of job descriptions. A gesture is sometimes made in the direction of relatedness and structure by putting dotted lines on the organization chart, but these frequently serve to confuse rather than to clarify the issue.

In addition to job descriptions and organization charts in a company, there are other elements such as budgets, forms, appraisal systems, systems for introducing new products to the company, salary-administration systems, long-range forecasts, management-development systems, goal-setting systems, data-processing systems, and management-information systems. All are developed independently with very little integration and frequently with an increasing despair on the part of those who are called upon to develop the systems, through the recognition of how little relevance or connection there is between what they are doing and what the rest of the company is doing.

The framework within which reorganization is at present undertaken is one in which *analysis*, or *reduction*, alone is known and recognized. This inadequate framework brings about a violation of harmony, of structure. "Everyone knows" that to solve a problem one must start by breaking the problem down into smaller problems and, where necessary, these into yet smaller problems. One then goes about solving each of these simple problems and then synthesizes or integrates the solutions in a steadily ascending hierarchy. However, to break a problem down is to reduce the level of the problem, and by changing its level one changes the problem entirely.

If we are to have a harmonious and integrated system, we must constantly bear in mind that a company is a whole, a total system. Nevertheless, it is a composite and multi-dimensional system.

To organize but part of the company is like trying to bake half a cake. Often a manager will say, "Well, first let us set up this and that department, or this and that role within the department, or perhaps this and that system. Let us get those working, and then later on we can turn our attention to the rest of the organization." This is something like a housewife saying, "Let us first of all put in the flour and water and perhaps some currants, and later on we will get around to the eggs and sugar and the rest of the ingredients, when we have cooked the first part of the cake."

Classical organization theory suggests that there is "the company" and that there is "change," and these two are in some way in opposition. Monolithic organizations have been set up with the view that the company acquires significance through its stability. Emphasis has been put on the hierarchical structuring, and a tendency toward "power structuring" has enabled the company to acquire inertia, or resistance to change. This inertia has a positive side in so far as it assists the company to face the forces of degeneration and deterioration. On the other hand, the emphasis on the hierarchic structuring of the company has inhibited the generation of ideas. It would be nearer the truth to say that an organization should be the orderly expression of change.

An organization changes along three "spatial" dimensions: lateral, horizontal, and vertical. Its functions become increasingly more differentiated and complex (the lateral dimension). New systems, procedures, and understandings bring about new integrations or new orientation, and there is a tendency toward different and new wholes to be created within a company (the horizontal dimension). The organization also changes in another dimension. As the company grows, higher level ideas are introduced, enabling it to encompass an increasing field of phenomena (the vertical dimension).

Change can occur at many different points within the system. The emphasis on the vertical dimension or the hierarchic structure tends to resist the influence of many of these changes. This results in the "cataclysmic" approach to reorganization according to which a company is organized at a given time and then, through a continuing failure to adapt, it reaches a crisis, at which point a new reorganization becomes necessary and the cycle is repeated. By regarding a company as a system open to its environment, having many dimensions, each of which is inducing change, the cataclysmic approach can be replaced by a more dynamic approach based on *growth*.

In industry, "growth" commonly means but one thing: to get bigger. Success is equated with size, rationalized as economy of scale, and projected as a national faith through the G.N.P. index. Hollywood, Broadway, General Motors, and more recently the conglomerates are the result. A balloon, as it is blown up, gets bigger—but this is not growth. It is simply expansion. As many a breathless and startled reveler has discovered, bigger is not always better. The capacity of the balloon does not grow, but the capacity is subjected to more and more demands. Expansion could therefore be seen as using more and more of a given capacity. Growth, on the other hand, means increasing the capacity of the system as well as the demands that are made upon it. Partial reorganization of a company would bring about expansion or integration. Expansion occurs when the reorganization causes those parts of the organization that are addressed to increase their demands upon the rest of the system (for example, a new sales drive). Integration occurs when the reorganization enables parts of the system to interact more easily (for example, a work simplification program). Only total reorganization can bring about growth. Without growth the forces of differentiation and integration—process and structure—become unresolved conflict, causing fragmentation, empire building, and eventually the decline of the company.

We can therefore differentiate three forms of "orderly" change that can occur within a company:

1) The change of integration, which we shall call *self-regulation*.
2) The change of *expansion*.
3) The change called *growth*.

Philosophers have long been aware that our experience of the world is not simple but complex. A few moments' reflection will show most people that *what* we experience, *how* we experience it, *why* we experience it, and *that* we experience at all are different sides or dimensions of experience. What we experience gives rise to facts. How we experience gives rise to functions. Why we experience this rather than that gives rise to structure. *That* we experience at all gives rise to a mystery, related in some way to Will. *Will is the urge in everything toward self-realization.* Everything is pressing out toward being itself to the fullest. Everything seeks to express itself.[2] This self-expression arises through interaction of what we shall call *structure* and *process*. It also arises through two trends: one toward the center and the other toward the periphery; one toward greater depth, greater meaning, the other toward greater scope and more influence. The four interacting conditions (structure/process, center/periphery) give rise to being. As we shall show later, there is an inner contradiction among these four, and it is this very self-contradiction that gives rise to the permanency and stability of being. *Being is the inner-togetherness[3] of forces that manifest in opposition.* Function is the outcome of these forces striving to become one in the urge toward self-realization. In Will, the how and the why are unified in understanding and growth. In growth, the three find fulfillment of their possibilities.

This is true also of a company. There are three forces at work within a company: the forces known as "shareholder," "market," and "employee." An organization is a truly wonderful expression of these three interacting forces[4] within a unity or whole that find expression and realization in growth. Growth, not profit, is the real significance of corporate life.

We cannot view a company simply as an instrument by which profit (that is, return to the shareholder) is maximized. This univalent view does not agree with the facts. Those who defend the profit concept rightly point out that if a company does not make a profit—that is, if it does not satisfy the needs of the shareholder—then the shareholder will withdraw his support and the company will decline. However, this power to withdraw support also rests with the employee and with the customer. Should the support of either of these be withdrawn, the results would be as serious as should the shareholder withdraw his support. There is, therefore, a triad of forces or role systems.

Wilfred Brown, chairman of a large industry in Britain, who has written quite extensively on management and organization from the point of view of a practicing manager, has said:

> One of the features of each of these role systems is that they possess very considerable power, vis-à-vis the company. The . . . systems are as follows: *A group of shareholders,* who elect directors to represent them, who in turn appoint the chief executive and set policies within which he can operate the company.
>
> *A group of customers*—it may seem far-fetched to refer to them as a role system, but I think an analysis will show that it is justified. Individually they certainly possess considerable power vis-à-vis the company. They can, in fact, close it down if they dislike, say, its products, prices, delivery dates, by withdrawing their custom.
>
> *The representative system* (i.e., the employees) comprising everybody in the company . . . They possess great power and can *in extremis* close the company down by going on strike.[5]

These forces, although quite different from one another, have an equality of status within an organization. All three are investors.

A shareholder invests money because he has money to invest, and seeks for the highest return with the lowest risk possible. The shareholder also wishes to see his investment grow over the years and will sometimes be prepared to receive a relatively low immediate return from the investment in the form of dividends if he feels confident that it will be balanced by a fairly high growth rate. It may be true that a shareholder is able to remove his investment at will, but when this investment represents very large sums of money, it can often mean movement at a loss, and it is movement that would require a considerable amount of study and application. So much so is this the case that financial analysts, who are the counterpart of employment placement centers, are sometimes called upon for assistance to make the move easier. Management is passing into the hands of professional managers; likewise financial investment is passing to an increasing degree into the hands of professional investors, and a professional investor *must find* an outlet for his investment.

An employee invests his capacity and ability in a company. He also has his expectations, which include a fair return for the work that he does, as well as a continually developing career. Once again, he may elect at some time to receive lower wages in order to acquire growth over the long term. He, like the investor in shares, is capable of moving his commitment. This movement may be made by changing jobs, but it also may be made by reducing his commitment to the work that he is required to do and increasing his commitment to some activity outside the company, such as service clubs, further study, local politics, and so on. Much of the work that is done in a company, particularly at the higher levels, requires fairly intense and continuous commitment. Without this, little can be accomplished. Unless the employee sees some satisfaction in what he is doing, this intense application and commitment will not be made. Yet it is out of just this application and commitment that the company grows in such a way that it is able to satisfy the needs of the shareholder.

If, therefore, we are to say that a company is in business to make a profit for the shareholders because otherwise the shareholders will withdraw their support and therefore cause the company to decline, we should likewise say that a company is in business for the well-being of the employees, and unless this need is met the employees will withdraw their commitment and the company will decline.

However, a third force must be reckoned with—that of the market. The market represents the *need* that society has for the continued existence of the company. The expectations of the market are for a quality product at a price that is reasonable. The market will also balance short-term against long-term considerations in the same way that the employees and shareholders make such considerations. If the market does not get its needs satisfied in one way, it will seek alternative ways. This is the same as saying that the market invests or commits its need to a particular company in anticipation that this need will be satisfied. If the company fails to provide that satisfaction, then commitment is withdrawn. There is a certain amount of inertia or inelasticity within the market, as there is among shareholders and employees, when it comes to change. The man who has bought some equipment that requires specialized parts is, in a way, a captive market for the company selling the equipment. But the market does have flexibility and can change its commitment, and this change in itself can be, of course, an important cause for the decline of a company.

The market is also becoming an increasingly "professional" one. In place of the corner store manager, chain stores have developed that are professional buyers of goods, wielding considerable purchasing power. The automobile industry sells much of its products to fleet owners and to people operating specialized equipment—once again a professional market. In addition to this, with the rise of consumerism and the various government bureaus dedicated to ensuring that the customer's rights are protected, the private market itself is becoming professionalized.

Each of these three—shareholder, employee, and market—makes a particular type of commitment. The shareholder *commits* money, which is the symbol of the social will; the employee *commits* his skills and know-how; the market *commits* need. What is important, therefore, is that in the first place a commitment is made, and in the second that this commitment is of a particular kind.

Commitment is an act of Will, and the company arises out of this act. Will is the urge to self-realization, and therefore *companies arise out of the urge to self-realization of the market, employees, and shareholders*. This is tantamount to saying that a company arises out of the urge to self-realization of the society of which that company is a part. Thus, the fundamental reason for a company being a company is to be found in Will.

It is through the shareholder that society sanctions what the company wishes to do. Society says, "Yes, you may do that," when money is invested in a company. Perhaps the principal difference between a free and socialist economy is the mechanism by which this social assent or commitment is made. In a controlled economy, a central authority says, "Yes, you may come into business, you may start production on that." But in a free economy there is a much more sensitive, a much more subtle medium by which society gives its consent. The stock exchange is an extremely sensitive instrument by which society is constantly making judgments on what is occurring in the industrial and commercial world. Wall Street may not be a very good judge if "good" means having high ethical standards, but it is an extremely sensitive judge. It is very quick to register approval or disapproval for changes within a company and within society at large.

The market, through the purchase of products, also gives assent to a company. The assent of a shareholder is, "Yes, you may do that." The assent that the market gives is, "Yes, you may do that, and with this result, or for this reason." The employee also gives assent when he says, "Yes, you may do this, and this is how it will be done. This is the quality it will be given."

It can be seen, therefore, that the market answers "why" in a company. The organizational structure of a company must conform to the market it has to serve—that is, to the product it has to produce. The employees answer the "how" in a company. The organizational processes of a company must conform to the abilities of the employees. The shareholders say *that* a company will be. The interaction of these three gives rise to a system, a set of independent but mutually related terms. The shareholder, the market, and the employee are independent role systems, but they are mutually related. They exist as independent elements of a single unified will that emerges from the common will to be. *A company is therefore a unity, a whole; but it is a composite and multidimensional whole, being the interaction of three forces.*

If a shareholder holds a million shares while another shareholder holds but ten, then it is more important to have the assent of the first than of the second. Likewise, if one customer purchases a thousand items and another customer but one, it is more important to have the assent of the first customer than of the second. Differences of magnitude can occur along a given dimension and give rise to different consequences. However, it is pointless to ask which of the three elements is the most important one. Each has its own legitimate expectation. Each strives to maximize the return that it gets from the company in which its commitment is invested. Each, therefore, strives to be the one of which the other two are expressions. This is the essence of the company system. To put the shareholder in a permanently dominating situation is to turn the system into an exploitive rather than an economic system.

2. THE BASIC TRIAD AS A FIELD

The three "commitments" of the shareholder, market, and employee can be looked upon as forces that make up the "field" of the company. Out of this field, or behavior space, arises the product, and it is from this product that a return on investment can be provided to shareholder, employee, and market for the investment that each makes.

The notion of the company as a field is a very important one for our study because in the first place it encourages a view of the company as a dynamic set of interacting forces, and secondly, it implies that the company is not a *thing,* nor simply a collection of *things.* A collection of things cannot grow (in the way that that term can best be used). Things can be added to the collection, but it is only when the interaction, the mutual relevance of these things is also taken into account, and, furthermore, when these interactions increase both in number and in complexity that growth can be considered to have taken place. The notion of a field[1] allows for these interactions to be taken into account. It allows for a qualitative understanding based on the notions of "fitness," order, harmony, emergence, and balance. Furthermore, and perhaps this is the most important, when the company is seen as a dynamic field of forces in equilibrium an orderly expression of change is possible.

The field theory is the Western counterpart of the Buddhist idea of Karma. From the Buddhist viewpoint there are no "things," no enduring entities, but rather each "thing" is seen to be a nexus of interacting causes and effects. This view of the world as a field will arise if the more familiar "dualistic" view of the world is given up. Our understanding of corporate life is bedeviled by dualities or *dichotomies,* by "either/ors": management/

men, staff/line, centralized/decentralized, skilled/unskilled, shareholders/employees, and so on. In what follows, an alternative to this dualistic view will be suggested for this dualism gives rise to so much of the frustration, sense of futility, and indeed destructiveness of our present way of behavior.

The interaction of the three forces can be shown in a diagram:

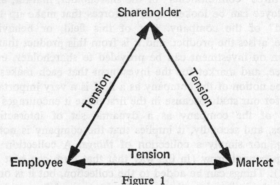

Figure 1

These three forces are not static. Each is in opposition to the others and yet each is dependent upon the others. Each seeks to maximize its returns: The customer seeks to get the best possible bargain for his commitment—he will look for the best quality at the cheapest price; the employee will seek to ensure that he gets the best conditions in terms of pay and challenge; the shareholder will look for the most secure growth and best dividends. The company, therefore, tends to lose its market, employees, and shareholders as they have a tendency to be attracted elsewhere to other means by which to get the maximum return. This pull from outside gives an outward direction to the dynamism of the forces.

Were this the whole story, a company could not stay in business for even a moment. However, the forces are not only in competition—in opposition—the forces are also complementary; they mutually support each other and thus there is a tendency toward the center.

The outward tendency has its basis in the need for each to improve its financial position in opposition to the others. This is not a conscious opposition, but as each seeks to maximize its financial benefits and because *at any one time* there is only so much finance, each necessarily opposes the others. The centering tendency has as its basis the need that each has for another kind of benefit.

The employee does not only have a need for higher pay; he also has a need for challenge, recognition, and personal growth. The customer does not only want something that is cheap, he also wants something that has quality, that will last and that has pleasing features. Likewise, the shareholder not only seeks dividends, but also wishes to see his investment grow—some shareholders even wish to see their investment grow in an enterprise worthy of growth.

The centering tendency is realized in the product of the company. It is the product that holds a company together and each of the forces collaborate to produce the product. Once again this collaboration is not a "conscious" one, but as each seeks to maximize its "centering" needs, a product comes into being. Our diagram can now be expanded thus:

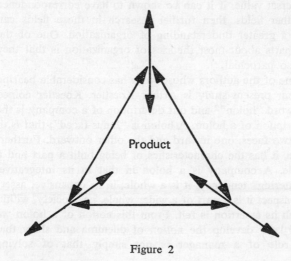

Product

Figure 2

Figure 2 shows a set of interacting forces. Some tend toward the center. These are the integrative forces; the forces of survival. They are the manifestation of the unity of Will. Those that tend toward the periphery manifest the expression of Will. Everything is pressing out to being itself to the full. This "pressing out," this "expression" in a company, gives *process;* the unity, the being itself, is the *structure.* From the balanced, harmonious dynamism of these forces comes growth. The tendency toward disintegration by explosion that arises from the centrifugal forces is balanced by a tendency toward destruction by implosion arising from the centripetal forces. As we shall see later, the exploding tendency is counteracted by the product; the imploding tendency is counteracted by the organizational structure.

In order to give our study a wider meaning, we shall be relating some of our findings to the work of several authors. If what we say about an organization just happens to be an accidental view, a view without counterpart elsewhere, then it may have a certain pragmatic value and that would be all. If, however, it can be shown to have a more universal value, if it can be shown to have correspondence in other fields, then further research in those fields can give a greater understanding of organization. One of the sad parts about most theories of organization is that they are so parochial.

One of the authors whose work has considerable bearing on our present study is Arthur Koestler. Koestler coined the word "holon"[2] and our description of a company is the description of a holon. A holon is "Janus-faced"; that is, it has two faces, one inward and the other outward. Furthermore, it has the characteristics of being both a part and a whole. A company is a holon in that in its integrative, "centering" tendency, it is a whole; in its expansive, assertive aspect it is a part of a wider whole, i.e., society, within which its assertion is felt. From this notion of a holon we shall later develop the notion of dilemma and show that the role of a manager is not simply that of solving problems, but also of resolving dilemmas. We shall therefore be returning again to the holon and its characteristics.

We have said that the opposition and collaboration between the forces is not on a conscious level and so far we have pictured two sets of "blind" forces at work. They are forces operating in the dark and are really forces in *potential*. A *third force* is necessary to make this potential a reality. This third force is to be found in the *role* of the president. The role of the president allows the forces to meet in a conscious way. The work of the president is to balance the forces at work in a company, and he does this by reconciling the conflict inherent in the opposing tendencies of the field through organization and what is known as "long range planning." The first counterbalances the explosive tendency; the second, the implosive tendency.

Included in the requirement to reconcile the polarity of the holon is the requirement to balance the claims of the three forces—shareholder, market, and employee—so that the commitment of each is retained. These are not two requirements—one being to reconcile the polarity and the other to balance the forces—but two different ways of viewing the same phenomenon.

3. A QUESTION OF OWNERSHIP

The standard view of a company could be called a "univalent" one: a linear descent from the board of directors through the managers and employees to the customer. This univalent view has as its corollary the belief that a company is "simply in business to make a profit." This belief is one of the most fundamental in the credo underlying the free enterprise system and needs to be examined carefully.

In general, there is a misunderstanding about who owns the company. Most people believe that shareholders own the company. But do they in fact do so? Or do they own shares in a company? This is a very important question because on the way it is answered rests the understanding that can be had of a company. To own implies to be able to control and to be responsible for. "Ownership-responsibility-control" are interdependent. Do shareholders control a company, are they responsible for what it does? It might be said in so far as the shareholders elect the board of directors and the board of directors selects the president that the shareholder indeed is in control. But is this the best way to account for the facts? For example, J. K. Galbraith[1] says that the annual meeting of the large business corporation is perhaps a most elaborate exercise in popular illusion because with great unction and little plausibility, corporate ceremony seeks to give the stockholder an impression of power. When the entrepreneur owned the company he shared this ownership with a few powerful shareholders, who ran the company with him. There was comparatively little pomp and ceremony. But as the stockholder gets less power, more ceremony is required.

The decline of power, moreover, is not confined simply to the shareholder but, according to *Business Week,* has extended to the board of directors. Even the board, which once sat at the right hand of the source of all economic power, must change its role. Its control is now becoming control in theory rather than in practice. "One of the totems of business is the board of directors. That august body, once synonymous with power, prestige, and probity, is now under attack. Its critics call it an ornamental anachronism and charge that board members no longer protect the interests of stockholders."[2] It seems that boards merely rubber stamp what managers have already decided, and can protect the interests of shareholders only when those interests coincide with those of the managers. "One company president, irritated that his directors did not give him total control, said: 'I didn't get to be president by soliciting a lot of opinions, then getting a consensus of everybody around, and going along with the majority—and that's one of the reasons our board has never really shaped up.'" A company director is reported to have said: "The reason I don't get involved as an outside board member is that I don't have time to get the facts, and I prefer not to look stupid. Silence is a marvelous cover."[3] It would further seem that "in most large and medium-sized companies where the president and board members own only a few shares of stock, the president determines what boards will do. In most cases this means that the board is relegated to performing functions that are substantially diluted from the classical roles of policymakers and guardians of the stockholders' interests."[4]

With a business run by an entrepreneur there is an owner, employees, and customers, with the entrepreneur being the owner. But with the professionalization of these three, the situation is different. It is no longer true to say that the shareholders own the company. Shareholders simply own shares. To "own" means to be able to control, as well as to have responsibility for, and although shareholders generally have a fair degree of ritual control, the real control of a company resides in the *role* of the president. A shareholder can control certain aspects of the financial dealings within a company, but the extent of this control is limited, as is the responsibility or liability he has for failure on the part of the company.

Although the meaning of ownership has changed in that it has become a much more complex notion than "this is mine and that is yours," the attitudes and beliefs that it once bred remain unchanged. To change these attitudes would need a prodigious exercise of thought and will, and it is easier and more comfortable—at least on the surface —to leave well enough alone. But, paradoxically, to leave well enough alone in this case means considerable rationalization, frustration, and even chaos. It would not be so bad if those who performed the magic of turning Cinderella shareholders into Queens for a Day were not taken in by their own magic; but they are.

One of the most pervasive dichotomies affecting our thinking and arising out of the univalent view is the management/employee dichotomy. A great deal of confusion has been created by this dichotomy because it naturally implies that managers are not employees. This implication is reinforced when managers discuss employees: "All that employees really want is as much money for as little work as they can get." "A company is not there for the good of its employees." And so on. When a manager says this, he is talking about *them*—the employees—not himself.

But the question naturally arises that if the manager is not an employee, what is he? This is where the shareholder-owner illusion becomes useful. Given the polarity "owner/employees" managers gravitate toward the "owners" as their source of power. This reinforces the belief in the univalent view of organization. Power, it is said, is vested at the top and percolates unidimensionally through the organization. This gives rise to the great emphasis that is put on the "organization chart" with the board of directors, and frequently even the shareholders, at the top.

This confusion about ownership furthermore distorts the

function of the role of the president. A manager is an employee. However, strictly speaking, the *president is not an employee: It is he who employs.* The role of the president is to put to use the commitment of employees, shareholders, and customers.

To understand fully the implications of what is being said, a distinction must be drawn between the *role* of the president and the person filling that role. The role of the president is independent of the board of directors; it is not something that is created, but arises out of the total field. This role is necessary in order that the three forces, one of which is represented by the board, may stay in equilibrium and so allow the whole field to grow. These three forces have equal status within the total field. Growth will be accomplished provided that the appropriate action is taken to meet the situations that arise. However, a distortion in the field is created because the *role* is filled by someone appointed by the board of directors—by one of the forces within the field. As well as being appointed by the board, he is also conditioned to respond to the needs of the board by bonuses, stock options, and other profit-oriented rewards. This means that the primary allegiance of the president-as-person will be to the board of directors, while the president-as-role requires equal allegiance to all three forces.

Because the president is appointed and can be dismissed by the board of directors, and because his attention is conditioned to the needs of the stockholder, a fundamental distortion is introduced into the field. Instead of being completely free within the options and as a consequence being able to adapt action perfectly to the requirements of the situation, most presidents are fixed, their strategy inflexible, their responses preconditioned. From the viewpoint of good organization—that is, the viewpoint on which company survival, effectiveness, and growth is based —different alternatives must be balanced and traded off, and these alternatives include, but are not equivalent to, profit maximization. But from the point of view of the president-as-person, only one strategy is acceptable: that which will maximize profit.

Ernest Dale says[5] that presidents, faced with the need to balance alternatives who act in a way to optimize the return for the different forces making up the field, find that they are unable to act at all. He is right in saying this since he is talking about the president-as-person, not the president-as-role. Dale is also right when he says that it is not surprising to see that many presidents find the only way out is to act irrationally, and this irrationality eventually pervades the entire organization.

The point of view we have developed so far assists in reconciling the various conflicting points of view of management theories. First, there is a divergence of opinion about which of the three primary elements is pre-eminent. Professor Dale's view, which is the one held, or at least expressed, by most businessmen and business theorists, is that the primary task of a company is to make a profit for the shareholders. Peter Drucker's viewpoint is different: For him the primary task of a company is to produce a product and fulfill a particular role in society. Just as Dale feels that the objective of providing a return on investment is an *ethical* obligation, Drucker feels that the objective of serving society through the market is also an ethical obligation. Drucker also tends to dismiss or play down the importance of the employees' needs and wants. "The large business organization does not exist for the sake of the employees. Its results lie outside and are only tangentially affected by employee approval, consent and attitude."[6]

For Galbraith, on the contrary, the company exists for the employees; that is, the technostructure: ". . . the association of men of diverse technical knowledge, experience, or other talent which modern industrial technology and planning require. It extends from the leadership of the modern enterprise down to just short of the labor force."[7] No doubt there would be a sufficient number of union leaders who would want to know why Galbraith stops "just short of the labor force." Galbraith does not believe the company is ethically obliged to serve the market or the shareholder. On the contrary, "so far from being controlled by the market, the firm to the best of its ability has made the market subordinate to the goals of its planning."[8] Galbraith is equally categoric when he says that profit maximization is no longer necessary.

The second difference in management theory is exemplified in the writings of Drucker and Galbraith. Drucker says, "Organizations do not exist for their own sake, they are a means; each is society's organ for the discharge of one social task. Survival is not an adequate goal for an organization as it is for a biological species. The organization's goal is a specific contribution to individuals and to society. The test of its performance, unlike that of a biological organism, therefore always lies outside of it."[9] For Galbraith the primary purpose of an organization is to survive: "For any organization, as for any organism, the goal objective that has a natural assumption of pre-eminence is the organization's own survival."[10] We may well ask who is right.

Within the framework of the theory being proposed, both are right: Galbraith is viewing the organization as structure, Drucker is viewing the organization as process. Galbraith, in fact, coined the word "techno*structure*" and it is significant to note that he did not coin the word "techno*process*." Drucker, on the other hand, developed management by objectives, which is essentially a process-oriented type of management. We have seen that the company must be viewed as a holon and that there are two tendencies at work: an integrative or survival tendency and an assertive or mission tendency. The conflict between Drucker and Galbraith can be shown to be simply one of point of view.

4. MANAGEMENT BY PRODUCT

That a company is a holon is reflected in what the employees, shareholders, and customers seek from their interrelationship. What they seek is also ambivalent. The employee, for example, wants to be part of the productive team, he wants challenge; but he also wants to be unique and seeks recognition to prove his uniqueness. The shareholder wants security of and growth in his investment; but he also wants high dividends. The customer wants a high-quality product that will satisfy his needs; but he also wants low prices. We shall deal more precisely with these polarities later, but for the moment let us recognize that it is through the *product* that the first set of needs (challenge, growth, and quality) may be satisfied, while it is through organization that the second set may be satisfied. Let us now, therefore, give our attention to the product.

Take for example a roughly cut, wedge-shaped piece of wood. Now let us ask ourselves whether this is a *product*. Most people, if they were asked this, would say no, because it is useless and no one would want it. If they are pressed, however, someone will likely seize on its shape and suggest that it could be used as a doorstop, and that if it were somewhere where there was plenty of wind and doors, indeed it could be a product. Dime stores sell rubber ones only slightly more elegant than our wedge of wood, and they are products. Let us consider this example for a moment and ask ourselves at what point the wedge of wood changed its character from a useless object to a product. It was when *an idea was introduced*.

A product is *an idea in a form*. In the case of the doorstop, the material out of which the form is made is not very important—it can be of wood, metal, rubber, or plastic—but the idea is constant: a wedge-shaped something that can be pushed under a door. But our definition of a product as an idea in a form is not complete. It was only when the block-of-wood-that-could-be-a-doorstop was put into juxtaposition with doors and wind—in other words when a *demand* was envisaged—that the block of wood truly took on the characteristics of a product. A product is therefore *an idea in a form with a demand*.

An idea *reveals* relations between phenomena, as opposed to a fact that could be said to *express* those relations. The idea is the center of gravity of the field in which it is perceived. The best analogy would be a center of light. The "form" of a product corresponds to the expression of relations revealed by an idea. Ideas alone are in demand, and old-time salesmen knew that they should "sell the sizzle and not the steak." Wherever one looks there are ideas that have been put into forms that have a demand: a pen, a desk, a room, or a building were originally ideas conceived by a man. Some of these ideas subsume a great number of other ideas. A car, for instance, subsumes thousands of ideas, including those that are expressed by the engine, the car body, the transmission, and the wheels, as well as those that are expressed in traffic laws, maps, and roads.

Some ideas can be specifically traced to their origin, others cannot. Where was the idea of a wheel first perceived? Who perceived a tie as being suitable apparel? The building you are in would have been conceived by an architect; the automobile was first designed by an engineer. Bell first perceived the telephone and Edison the electric light bulb. Whether or not the author is known, the idea originated with man.

It is through form that an idea becomes "something." Man fixes his idea in matter through energy, space, and time, or in the expectations of others, and so "expresses" his idea. This expression imposes limits upon the idea, isolates it, separates it from all others, and so makes it "a thing."

Looked at this way it becomes difficult to find the boundaries of an object. An automobile melts into subsuming and interacting ideas of steel, rubber, gasoline; ideas of friction and compression; ideas of fleets of cars, tanks, and jeeps; ideas of vacations, business trips, and visits to friends. An automobile is a system of ideas—ideas that stand in mutual relation with each other while retaining their integrity. Ideas reveal endless relations between phenomena expressed in form in a beginningless and endless flux.[1]

The definition of a product emphasizes the importance of the idea. It should be noted that an idea can only be directly perceived, or better still, *what is perceived is only perceived through the idea.* Zen has a saying that admonishes one not to confuse the finger that points to the moon with the moon itself; an eye cannot see itself.

Anything that can be said about the idea is not the idea, but an *expression* of an idea about the idea. A point comes when undertaking a descriptive analysis of experience, where words fail and all that can be done is to shrug one's shoulders or wave one's hands. Words are but the skin of reality, not its muscles or nerves. It must be accepted that certain concepts are almost undefinable, and among such undefinable concepts is an "idea."

It may, however, be useful to say what the concept "idea" is not meant to convey. It must not be construed as in opposition to some greater reality, something more substantial like a rock, a brick, or a pile of gold. It is different from thought. A thought may be the way in which an idea finds expression, but an idea can also find expression through music, painting, dancing, gestures, symbols, and so on. It is not to be found separate from experience. In other words, it is not a "spiritual" or "mystical" thing that floats in some unworldly ether. It is not something that "one can be conscious of." It is neither unique nor general, and the words "it" and "something" are used above only as an admission of failure. The idea is not, however, nothing. The very coherence of the world depends upon the idea that reveals to us the relationships of this world.

The notion of idea is, of course, very important philosophically, and many philosophers have struggled to define it unequivocally. The notion is, nonetheless, of practical importance in the world of commerce and industry. *The level of a product, and therefore of a company, is a function of the level of the idea of which that product is the expression.* Furthermore, the potential for growth that a company has is directly related to the level of the primary product of that company. In a well-known article[2] it is pointed out that the railroads stopped growing even though the need for transportation increased. This did not occur because the need was filled by others, but simply because it was not filled by the railroads themselves. The railroads let others take customers away from them because "they assumed themselves to be in the railroad business rather than in the transportation business. The reason they defined their industry wrongly was because they were railroad-oriented instead of transportation-oriented." Hollywood also perceived its business incorrectly and suffered as a consequence. "It thought it was in the movie business when it was really in the entertainment business. 'Movies' implies a specific limited product" (i.e., lower level idea).[3]

Peter Drucker underlines the importance of what we are saying when he asks, "Is a company that makes and sells kitchen appliances, such as electric ranges, in the food business? Is it in the homemaking business? Or is its main business really consumer finance? Each answer might be the right one at a given time for a given company. But each would lead to very different conclusions as to where the company should put its efforts and seek its rewards."[4] The answer depends upon the idea.

It is only incidental to the manufacturing process that material so frequently provides the form. Modern industry is seeing a rapid increase in work directed simply to expressing ideas in verbal form. With the change to power through influence with its concomitant change to professionalism, the expression of ideas in verbal form will become increasingly important. Much of the work done at middle and senior management level, much of the consultation work, is simply the expression of ideas in a verbal form through reports, financial statements, contracts, and decisions. The result that ensues from the work of a financial, engineering, or industrial relations consultant is no less a product than the result of a heavy steel worker or an automobile engineer. A medical diagnosis is a product, and so is a lecture. A lecture may be written or given orally, it may be fixed in some laboratory apparatus, or given incidentally to the process of constructing, maintaining, or operating a machine. In any case, it is a product as we have defined the word.

Materiality is but one way to make an idea endure; ideas are also captured by the mind through language. A word is an idea in a form with a demand. Words are products, and just as one product subsumes another product, so some words or elements of language subsume others.*

Normally the economist does not consider banking as a product. It is considered a service. But this service is still an idea in a form with a demand. The idea is that there should be readily accessible finances, and the form is that of the check, the bank statement, the overdraft, etc. The term "product" will therefore be used to cover the full range of the expression of an idea in a form with a demand and will include those services that a bank, insurance company, or a hotel provide.

---

* A fact is the expression of an idea; it is that which arises when the idea has been limited by matter, energy, space, and time. We are inclined to believe that a fact is a mental construct only, yet it is well to remember that the word "fact" is derived from the Latin *"facere,"* which means "to do" or "to make." From *facere* is also derived the French word *"fait,"* which means "do," "make," and "fact." What a man makes or does derives from the idea that he perceives. All the artifacts of men are in a way "facts." The manufacturing that a man originally did consisted of expressing the idea through fact by hand (In Latin, *manus* means "hand"). With the rise of capitalism, machines have taken the place of hands, but manufacturing is still basically the expression of an idea through a form even though it occurs in factories rather than in studies.

The form that a product takes is given by the material, equipment, and components of the company. These are provided by the shareholder dimension. The form represents the cost of the product. The form of the product is, therefore, the commitment of the shareholder in action.

But a product is not simply an idea in a form. There must be a demand for the idea before it can be said to be a product, and this is provided by the customer. It is a *form* that frames the evanescence of an idea, but it is *demand* that makes it real. By demand we mean need, with the willingness and ability to work, i.e., pay, to have the need satisfied. Through demand the form meshes or fits in with other forms. Through demand a link or interchange is established between the company-as-product and its environment.

The recognition of the product as an idea in a form with a demand, and therefore of the idea being "the central and dominating value" in a company, puts the total human being back into the industrial scene. The perception and realization of an idea is the employee dimension in action. "A business devoted to the identification of central ideas, the formulation of strategies for moving swiftly from ideas to operations, will differ in structure and activity from a company primarily concerned with management of money or physical resources."[5]

Undoubtedly the major concern in industry to date has been with materials handling. "Human relations" has been addressed to a very large degree to ensuring that people do not get in the way of the material. But to survive in the future the problem for industry will be increasingly one of idea generation. A company could be looked upon as an organism whose primary food is ideas. Ideas originate along the employee dimension. Strictly speaking, however, it will not do to say that men "create" the idea. Man's creativity is realized in the expression of the idea, in "pressing out" the idea, and so making it fact.

Management by idea is a broader concept than management by objective, or long-range planning. In some of the more advanced industries, top management has defined a "core idea" around which total company effort can be designed, such as "a shift in the definition of a business from one concerned with the sale of a product to one concerned with the delivery of a complete system of customer values —as in airlines marketing packaged vacations and computer manufacturers marketing systems to solve customers' information problems."[6] Each of these ideas is the energized core of a unique design for a business. The exploitation of each idea requires a comprehensive intellectual grasp of the totality of a business viewed as an interacting system." The task demands "special intellectual ability to *visualize* the translation of ideas and strategies into controlled operating systems responsive to dynamic change"[7] (author's italics).

5. STRUCTURE/PROCESS

So far it has been said that a company is a system, i.e., a set of interacting forces, and that it is a field in dynamic equilibrium that finds its expression through an idea in a form with a demand. This combination of a field and a set of interacting forces is the organization.

The word "organization" can be used in several ways. It means the relationship between people and things when doing work. It also means the right sequence of events. A well-organized situation has a *structure* of rules, methods, and procedures that are known and mutually support each other. The good organizer, on the other hand, is someone who gets a *process* moving on time with the minimum of delays and crises. Thus, in organization there is both a structural and process dimension. However, although these two dimensions are distinct, *they are not separate.*

Most thinkers oppose structure to process. For example, the question is often asked whether structure monitors process or process monitors structure. Traditionally, modern science has emphasized process in contrast to the ancient Greeks, for example, who emphasized structure. This structure-process opposition has dominated our thinking in the West and has fostered the religion-science dichotomy, with religion favoring structure and science favoring process. In industry this same conflict exists and is brought out in the denigration of the bureaucrat and the exaltation of the aggressive, result-oriented executive.

If we are to have an understanding of organization that will enable us to set up situations in which growth, as well as expansion and self-regulation, can occur, we must understand that we cannot oppose these two and therefore must come to terms with the polarity of structure and process. We shall therefore explore this problem at length to show some of the elements that have to be taken into account. The limitations of our habitual way of thinking about things will be exemplified by the difficulty of truly expressing this not-two, not-one aspect of the company, and we shall see that this has very far reaching effects.

The physical scientists are also having to come to terms with this polarity of structure and process, and one leading scientist who sees this need goes so far as to say, "Before the doctrine of reciprocal causal interaction between particle and field can possess meaningful, consistent theoretical formulation a new theory of the first principles of science must be developed."[1] However, there is a more fundamental requirement even than this. We have to change the very structure and process of our thinking. We have to change the very principles on which our thinking is based and the way that we think.

When working with an organization what is required is that we deal *at the same time* with structure and process, taking into account the simultaneity of structure and the sequence of process. Not only this, we must at the same time be able to deal with the effect the changes in either of these have upon the other, themselves, and the situation as a whole. It is evident that by using our normal, conceptual equipment alone we just cannot do this. Even if we were able to produce a computer program that did not reticulate to infinity and were to give this problem to a computer, we should still have to assimilate the output.

But it is possible to deal with this situation at another level. This is unquestionably the case because managers *do* organize situations that remain viable and achieve results. But they do this by something other than concepts. Often they achieve their organization by a hunch, by a "seat-of-the-pants" approach. This approach has the failing of being uncertain and disruptive. It is disruptive simply because it is so difficult to communicate. Sometimes though another method is used, which is the constant application of intuition or "weighing," and it is this with which we are concerned here. With this approach, all the elements within the situation are allowed to maintain their full concreteness and yet at the same time be juxtaposed to other elements that may well be logically incompatible with them. The implications that this manifold of elements has are then allowed to find their own expression through the natural wisdom of the mind. This wisdom by its nature seeks simple and complete resolutions that are capable of being implemented. It is precisely in the development of this approach that Buddhism has so much to offer, emanating as it does just from this wisdom.[2]

Basic to the Buddhist outlook is polarity, and the fundamental polarity is form and emptiness. In Zen temples monks chant daily a *sutra*, the Prajna Paramita, which is the distillation of Buddhist teaching. Central to this *sutra* are the words: "Form is no other than emptiness; emptiness no other than form." Form is what we are calling "structure," emptiness is, in part, what we are calling "process." This statement, that form is no other than emptiness, does not mean that they can be reduced to one another, because structure is structure and emptiness is emptiness. This is bewildering to anyone first encountering the concept, but at the same time it often strikes a note of satisfaction.

This doctrine of form and emptiness is associated with another that we have referred to as not-two, not-one. Also associated with it are the concepts of the "middle-way" and "karma," two concepts that are badly understood in the West. The concept of karma has many levels of meaning; one level is associated with the doctrine of dependent origination, which has the underlying notion of "this being, that appears."[3]

These notions arise naturally out of our wisdom mind. It is not suggested, therefore, that we abandon Western thinking and adopt oriental thinking. Western thinking is, as we have said, process-dominated. It is, using Marshall McLuhan's phraseology, linear thinking. It is the sort of thinking that is inevitable in the absence of a discipline designed to bring about its complement. It sees things as being what they are because of the special properties or characteristics that they have. To learn Buddhist logic or philosophy as an academic subject would be a waste of time to any but the professional philosopher, particularly where that philosophy is made available by Western classical scholars steeped as they are in process thinking. What is suggested is that we rediscover the complementary discipline as a Western discipline, and this is entirely possible for us through Zen. To practice Zen we do not have to adopt or imitate Eastern life-styles at all.

The remarkable thing is that the modern business climate is the best climate within which this new way of thinking could take root and grow because it is both economically oriented and result oriented at the same time. We shall throughout the rest of the book be providing evidence in favor of this statement, and it is partly to lay the groundwork for this evidence that we shall pursue a presentation of the structure/process polarity and its implications. But this presentation is also offered because intrinsically it is a most important notion to anyone dealing with organization. We shall endeavor to show some of the consequences of industry's inability to come to terms with this polarity in a later chapter entitled "Staff and Line."

The structural dimension of an organization has a spacelike quality. Roles exist simultaneously "alongside" each other. In organization as process these same roles manifest themselves through task cycles and occur in sequence, in a timelike dimension. An organization can be looked at as a space/time or structure/process continuum. It is a holon with the structural dimension providing the survival mode and the process dimension providing the expressive mode. The structural organization and process organization are therefore not two separate organizations: They both involve the whole company and are not two halves of the company.

A role and a company are isomorphic. This can be readily seen if one compares a one-man business to a large company and realizes that all that is done in the company is also done in the one-man business. What is done as one task among many in the one-man business is done in a large company by a role or even a department. For example, the selling function is just one task carried out by the man in his own business, but is a role or a number of roles or a department in a company. Further evidence of the isomorphism of a role and company is given by the fact that what starts out as a task within a role may develop into a role, then a department, and finally may be subcontracted out to a company specializing in performing that one task. Examples of this having occurred abound in the automotive industry. This, furthermore, demonstrates that a task is also isomorphic with a role. A set of isomorphisms is therefore possible which include task, role, and company.

Isomorphisms within a systematic study are as important as equations in a mathematical study. Indeed, an equation could be considered as a special class of isomorphism. The value of isomorphism is that by understanding the interrelatedness of one system, a corresponding interrelatedness can be postulated for another system which is isomorphic with it. This is similar to transformation carried out in mathematics. For example, within a company there are six basic functions, three of which are structural functions and three process functions. These six functions may be carried out by one man or some or all of them may be delegated as roles to individuals. When they are delegated, the roles will also have a structural and process aspect and will also have six distinct but mutually related elements. When they are not delegated, the functions will remain as tasks, but these tasks in their turn will also have a structural and process dimension and will also have six elements.

A task cycle is made up of subcycles or elements and in its turn is part of a larger, supra cycle. The task cycle is the "atom" of the company. A whole company finds its focus in each task cycle that is accomplished and in turn is made up of all the task cycles that are occurring. A company is a whole task cycle and can be looked at as such. It is born of an idea, it grows as long as the idea is capable of being perceived as such, and it dies when the idea ceases. It is made up of a myriad of cycles and subcycles. To fully understand organization as process, it is necessary to fully understand what is meant by the expression "task cycle."

Task cycles may be carried out by individuals—for example, typing a letter—or by the company as a whole—for example, building an extension to the manufacturing plant. Both are task cycles. To help us further understand the concept, let us consider the work of a cobbler. When a cobbler makes a pair of shoes he first decides upon the shape, color, size, style, and so on. He then gathers together the various materials needed to make the shoes and manufactures them. They are then put on display and eventually sold to a customer. This is a task cycle.

In the above example it can be seen that a task cycle goes through various stages, in this case through the stages of deciding which type of shoes to make, manufacturing them, and selling them. These are three subcycles. The first subcycle is concerned with developing the product; the second, with processing or manufacturing the product; and the third, with linking the product to the customer. This task cycle with its subcycles could be depicted thus:

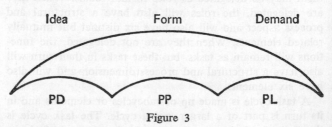

PRODUCT CYCLE

Idea   Form   Demand

PD   PP   PL

Figure 3

This analysis of a task cycle fits in with the definition of a product given earlier: an idea in a form with a demand. Product development coincides with the idea, product processing with the form, and product linking with the demand.

In developing the product, the idea is perceived; that is, the relations between phenomena are made known and the implications of expressing the idea are resolved. The idea is perceived within an "ideational," but nonetheless concrete, environment. In product development it is necessary to see the idea in its concreteness through the various modes of expression that are open. It could be said that in the product-development stage the idea is coalesced or merged in a viable whole with other ideas.

The product-processing stage is related to the form. In the product-processing phase the idea is coalesced with those materials suited to give it a form. Manufacturing is the expression of the idea. It is the process through which the idea is made fact.

The product-linking phase is related to demand. In the product-development phase the idea was coalesced with other ideas; in the product-processing phase it is coalesced with the materials to give it form; and in the linking phase it will be coalesced with need which will give it value or meaning.

A task cycle is obviously not "something"; we cannot point to it. If we should walk around a factory, we would simply see a total "ongoingness." In this ongoingness things are happening as a continuous process. This brings us to an important point, which is that we cannot reach structure through the senses. Whoever says that he only believes what he sees, will not believe in structure. But the very timing of process, the interaction and integration—now at this level and now at that level—of simultaneous but related processes is structure made manifest.

The task cycle we have defined is but an abstraction. We have shown it as an isolated cycle, as pure process. We must now show a task cycle as a holon, as a structure/process whole.

6. WORK AND ORGANIZATION

Since a task cycle is the "atom" of an organization, by focusing on the task cycle work is brought clearly into perspective. The company arises through work, is sustained by work, expands and grows with work. If the basic aims are to survive and to contribute, the means by which these aims are realized is work.

Some social scientists have emphasized the importance of the informal group and the satisfaction workers enjoy through belonging to them. For the organization analyst, however, the informal group could be considered "noise" within the system. The less well organized the company is in terms of accomplishing work, the greater will be the tendency for its members to seek satisfaction through informal groups.

Through work man is able to satisfy many of his needs. "When a man works he has a contributing place in society. He earns the right to be the partner of other men. The fact that someone will pay for his work is an indication that what he does is needed by others, and therefore that he is a necessary part of the social fabric. He matters—as a man. To have a skill, trade, or occupation is to be a 'who' and 'what.' "[1]

The accomplishment of work is also most important to the health of the company. The less efficiently a company produces its product—that is, the less effective the organization is—the poorer the organizational health and the weaker its constitution. This in turn will feed back onto the employees, through badly structured assignments and less challenge. Thus, if we are to understand the organization, we must understand work.

Even though work is so important in our lives, the word "work" has only recently been adequately defined. This lack of definition has inhibited any clear, formal communication between people about work. It is therefore impossible even to *begin* a discussion about organization that can hope to succeed. Managers who are asked to define work frequently consider it as "physical exertion," "the expenditure of time," "mental effort," "something that is done to accomplish some worthwhile result," or "putting things together." When one considers the physicist's clear definition of work as the force times the distance through which the force acts, it can be seen how poorly structured is management's thinking about that which is so important.

It is a matter of common observation that no one in a company is able to do as he likes. *Limits* are imposed at all levels and in all parts of a company, including that of the president. On the other hand, work implies some sort of *result*. Activity that does not produce a result is simply agitation. Thus we can see that work has something to do with getting results within limits.

Whereas the limits prescribe the activity of the person at work and the results direct his energies, nevertheless at all levels in an organization there is left to the worker the exercise of discretion. The meaning of this word "discretion" will be, for the moment, left open and will simply be considered to be "know-how"; later it will be explored and defined. Work can, therefore, be defined as the application of discretion within limits in order to produce a result. To give the full definition given by Elliott Jaques: *"Employment work is the application of knowledge and the exercise of discretion within limits prescribed by the immediate manager and by higher policies, in order to carry out the activities allocated by the immediate manager, the whole carried out within an employment contract for a wage or salary."* [2]

The definition of work as the exercise of discretion within limits in order to produce a result applies not only to human work, but to the work of anything that is alive. Koestler pointed out that "the common spider will suspend its web from three, four, and up to twelve handy points of attachment, depending on the lie of the land, but the radial threads will always intersect the laterals at equal angles, according to a fixed *code of rules* built into the spider's nervous system; and the center of the web will always be at its center of gravity. The *matrix*—the web building skill —is flexible: it can be adapted to environmental conditions; but the rules of the code must be observed and set a limit to flexibility. The spider's choice of suitable points of attachment for the web are a matter of *strategy*, depending on the environment, but the form of the completed web will always be polygonal, determined by the code. The exercise of a skill is always under the dual control: (a) of a fixed code of rules (which may be innate or acquired by learning), and (b) of a flexible strategy, guided by environmental pointers to the 'lie of the land.' "[3]

Koestler returned to this idea of strategies and rules in a later book and gave the notion a wider application: "Functional holons are governed by fixed sets of rules and display more or less flexible strategies. The rules—referred to as the system's *canon*—determine its invariant properties, its structural configuration and/or functional pattern. While the canon defines the permissible steps in the holon's activities, the strategic selection of the actual steps among possible choices is guided by the contingencies of the environment."[4]

To understand a task cycle it is first necessary to know the results it must attain. Many managers, when thinking about work—for example, when writing role descriptions —concern themselves with the various things that an employee in a role has to do, that is, the various activities he has to perform. There is no end to the things that a person has to do, and these things are invariably tied up with the application of discretion. Frequently the very things that are put into a role description are not indeed part of the role, but some of the alternative ways to reach the results expected.

The first thing, then, is to define the result. The result of work must have some use in the company and must be in some form that is acceptable. Furthermore, the company must be prepared to commit resources to achieving that result. We have defined a product as a result, in an acceptable form, that is needed and for which there is an ability and willingness to pay. Therefore, as all task cycles and, hence, roles must have one or more products, the definition of work will be expanded to "the exercise of discretion within limits in order to produce a *product*."

Limits are essential to do work. Without limits one would be unable to act at all. Many people are of the opinion that freedom lies in the absence of limits, but this is not so. The completely free man is, paradoxically, completely determined, in that he can only perform one single act in a given circumstance, that is, the act totally adequate to the situation.

The work generated in an internal combustion engine can serve as an illustration of what is meant. The cylinder walls are the limits, the moving piston is the result. The more perfectly the limits are adjusted to the result, the more efficient the operation will be. The whole point of an engine is to turn a shaft. This is done by a piston that goes up and down. This cannot be achieved without limits. If the walls of the cylinder do not fit the piston tightly enough, gas escapes and efficiency suffers. If the cylinder fits the piston too tightly, energy is wasted through friction, heat, and noise.

Limits have a further interest in so far as they have a recognizable structure that is repeated at all levels within a company, from the simplest function, such as a filing clerk, to the president of the company. This structure expresses itself in different ways, but basically it is the same structure at each level. We have said that there are different levels within a company. Now it can be said that one of the ways that this difference can be recognized is in the way that the limits find expression.

Let us first consider the simplest level and use as an example the work of a filing clerk. We shall call this the level of *function*. We shall differentiate between work and mere activity by the simple expedient of determining whether discretion is allowed within limits. If no discretion is allowed, if the limits are so fixed that there is no freedom to choose between alternatives and adjust to the choice made, then there is an activity, but no work.

A filing clerk is required to put reports, invoices, or other material into an existing system according to a specified code. Furthermore, the clerk is given this material in a random order. What are the limits involved? Another way of asking this question is, "How is the work to be judged?" Two criteria present themselves: (1) Has the clerk kept to the code; does the result of the work match the structure in which the work was done? The situation has a structure, and by matching what was done with the structure, the work acquires a certain *quality*, and this quality, that is required, can be made known. (2) Was the work done in the time allowed? This time allowance can also be made known to the clerk. Thus, the two primary limits are *quality* and *pace*, and the filing clerk is in a position to trade one of the limits against the other and so accomplish the work. The clerk is therefore judged on how *well* and how *fast* something is done.

Let us compare the work of a filing clerk with the work of a person working on a conveyor belt who is given a spanner that is so constructed that only a given pressure can be applied to a nut. This worker is unable to trade time against quality as both are fixed—the time is set by the conveyor, the quality by the spanner. The discretion of this worker is so limited that it could be considered as an activity but not a function. The inventive genius of production engineers has for years been devoted to delegating just this sort of activity in the belief that it would be efficient.

Work as opposed to mere activity requires discretion,

and discretion means the total human being in action; it means commitment of capacity and ability. But for work to exist, minimum limits of pace and quality, or minimum resources of time and structure, must be made available.

It rarely happens that an employee is just given one single task to perform. More frequently roles are multitask roles, that is, roles having more than one task cycle to complete. Often typing, answering the telephone, mailing letters, and other tasks are allocated to go along with filing tasks. A manager says, "Type this letter, answer the telephone when it rings, and if people call for information from these files, give it to them; and if you happen to see Mr. Brown go by, please give him this. . . ."

The clerk is therefore required to organize a system of machines, equipment, paper, and knowledge; that is, to bring these together within a framework of pace and quality and also priorities. Therefore, a new limit is presented and a new dimension appears. The typist has to determine priorities. This we shall call an *operation*, which is a higher level than a function described earlier.

At a higher level still the structural limits of the role not only include the structure inherent in the situation which is made known through the code or at higher levels through standard practices, policies, procedures, and so on, but also includes people. In other words, the structural limits are *organizational* as well as situational limits. Furthermore, the pace limit has an added dimension that is normally reflected in a discretionary budget or discretionary expenditure of some kind. In addition to priority, a further limit of *value* is added.

Most managers have a budget within which to operate. The more fortunate have an explicit budget; the less fortunate, an implicit one. A manager with an implicit budget is like a man who is asked to go to a wall with his eyes closed. He knows the wall is there, but he has to exercise a fair degree of caution in reaching it.

The organizational limits within which managers work are normally made explicit by way of organization structure, role descriptions, standard practice procedures, and so on.

The value limit is established by the product idea, which is determined by the needs of the company. Value and quality are distinct. Value relates the product to its environment. Quality relates to the relationship that parts of the product have between themselves. It is possible for a high-quality product to have low value. Likewise it is possible for a product of low quality to have a high value.

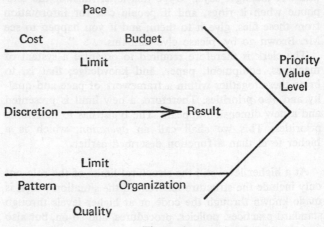

Figure 4

Quality and organization both have *pattern,* or inner interrelationship, in common. Pace and budget both have *cost* in common, and priority and value have *level* in common. Thus, the basic structure of limits governing all work is a cost-pattern-level structure.

The president's role can also be understood using this same paradigm. The president works within the limits set by the shareholder through a capital and operating budget, by the market through the company idea, and by the employees operating the organization as process and structure. Comparing the "cost/pattern/level" paradigm with the "shareholder/employee/market" paradigm, it can be seen that the shareholder enables the company to carry its cost, the employee enables the structure to be developed, and the market determines the value or level of the company.

In what we have said so far we have assumed that the task cycles within a company are in series, that is, one after the other. In the example of the cobbler it was said that the product-development phase precedes the product-processing phase, and this is followed by the product-linking phase. This, however, is an abstraction for two reasons. The first of these we have just dealt with. A task cycle is not just a process; it is not just a sequence of events. It is also a structure through the limitations within which it operates. We must now deal with the second reason and give greater concreteness to our understanding by pointing out that in the continuum of a company things do not simply occur one after another, they also occur simultaneously. Cycles not only occur in series, but also in parallel. It is because cycles occur in parallel that organization as structure is necessary.

Taking a stylized view of the automobile industry as an example, one can imagine that in a given year, say 1972, the cars for 1974 and subsequent years are being developed. Plans and designs would be drawn up and prototypes developed (PD). In that same year, 1972, the 1973 model would be manufactured (PP), while the 1972 model is being sold (PL).

Model year	Activities carried on in specific years				
	1971	1972	1973	1974	1975
1971	PL				
1972	PP	PL			
1973	PD	PP	PL		
1974		PD	PP	PL	
1975			PD	PP	PL

The cobbler carried out the task cycle within certain limits, and in the automobile industry these same limits are necessary. Any task cycle within the automobile industry is subject to them. However, we see that the product development, process, and linking cycles are going on simultaneously. What is now necessary is some way to relate these cycles in an integrated whole. Furthermore, it is necessary to be sure that what is created in one year has a market in a subsequent year and also that finance is available to provide equipment and resources necessary to produce the product and maintain the structure. This means that a new set of task cycles, having the same subcycles and limits as those involved in developing, processing, and linking the product come into being. These task cycles can also become roles and departments in the same way that such an evolution was seen to be possible for the other three task cycles. The product of these task cycles are the limits within which task cycles in a company are carried out.

It is now possible to follow the maturing of a company through its inception as a task cycle to a fully mature company that has six fully differentiated departments, each having a specific product related to the market, the manning and organization, the finance, the development of a product, the processing of a product, and the linking of a product.

The following diagrams illustrate our argument:

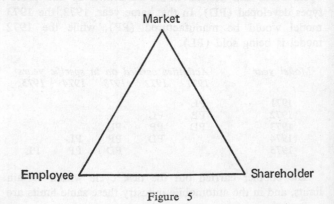

Figure 5

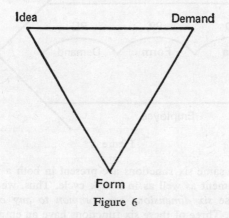

Figure 6

These can be combined in two ways:

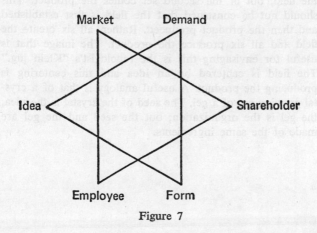

Figure 7

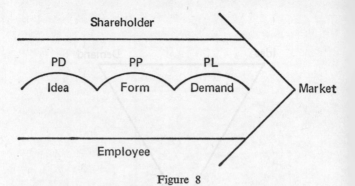

Figure 8

These same six functions are present in both a role and a department as well as in a task cycle. Thus, we can say that these *six dimensions are common to any economic function*. Three of these six functions have an emphasis on structure and three on process. Out of the first three comes the field, out of the second set comes the product. This should not be construed that the field is first established and then the product produced. Rather, all six create the field and all six produce the product. The image that is useful for envisaging this is the topologist's "Klein jug." The field is centered by an idea and this centering is producing the product. A useful analogy is that of a crystal growing out of a gel. The seed of the crystal is the idea, the gel is the organization; but the seed and the gel are made of the same ingredients.

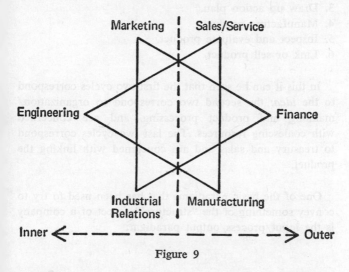

Figure 9

The six functions have a variety of names. In Figure 9 we have given what are probably the most common of them. The task cycle has six separate phases, which also have a variety of names.

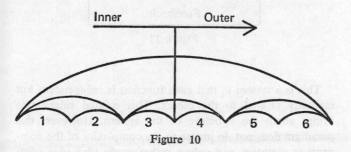

Figure 10

1. Identity need.
2. Design product.

3. Draw up action plan.
4. Manufacture product.
5. Inspect and evaluate product.
6. Link or sell product.

In this it can be seen that the first two cycles correspond to the *idea;* the second two correspond to organization/ manning and product processing, and are concerned with coalescing resources. The last two cycles correspond to treasury and sales and are concerned with linking the product.

One of the basic paradigms that has been used to try to convey something of the "structural" aspect of a company is the input/process/output paradigm:

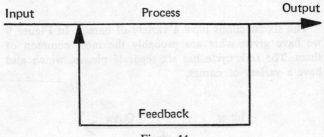

Figure 11

This is a system in that each function is independent but mutually related to the others. This mutual relatedness brings about the structure of the system. However, this paradigm does not do justice to the complexity of the company as a system and only a rather crude idea of a company at work can be derived from it.

What we have said so far can be better summed up in the following diagrams:

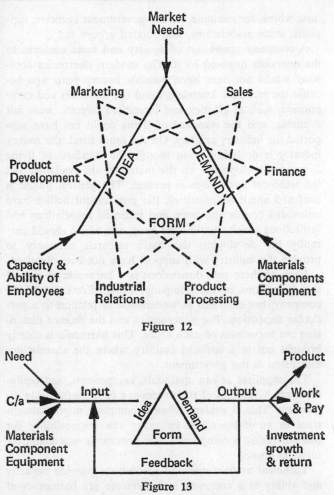

Figure 12

Figure 13

Before leaving the subject of the company as structure/process, we should complete the picture by pointing out some other forces that influence the company. The term "stakeholders" is beginning to have some popularity, and it might be asked where some of these fit into the picture; where, for example, do the government agencies, suppliers, trade associations, and related groups fit?

A company grows out of society and must conform to the restraints imposed by it. The modern electronics company would not have been possible twenty years ago because the technical knowledge and the materials and components, such as plastics and integrated circuits, were not available, and the standard of living could not have supported the industry anyway. On the other hand, the energy industry is declining, even though the standard of living demands development, all the materials are available, and the technical knowledge is present. The general public is confused about its priorities, the government bodies have outmoded boards and laws, and technical associations and institutions which should have been, and which should currently be, developing the basic research necessary to provide the industry with support have not been financed.

Each of these new dimensions is a harmonic of one of the dimensions of the company. Each affects the whole company, but each can be understood in relation to a particular dimension. The government and the finance dimension are harmonics of each other. This harmonic is clearly brought out in a socialist country where the shareholder dimension is the government.

The suppliers of raw materials, components, and equipment are harmonics of the processing or manufacturing dimension. This is evident when a company might subcontract to an independent company the responsibility for manufacturing a component that previously was manufactured in-house.

Technical associations and institutions provide capacity and ability to a company and therefore are harmonics of the personnel or capacity/ability dimensions. Universities interact with companies and provide valuable services in the form of research and consulting. In the gas industry, the American Gas Association and Canadian Gas Association supplement the capacity and ability of individual gas companies in a variety of ways.

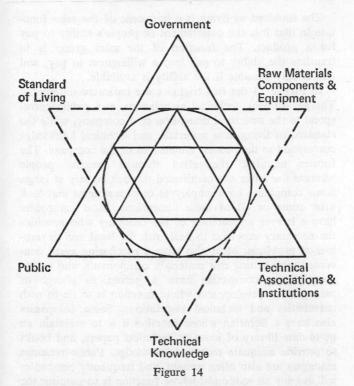

Figure 14

Technical knowledge is a harmonic of the product development group. It is available through magazines, books, seminars, and the personal interaction of like-minded people. Most companies recognize the importance of allowing their managers to have the opportunity of visiting other companies and attending conventions merely to make acquaintance with others in their particular profession.

The general public is a harmonic of the company's market. This is borne out quite clearly in the struggle that often arises between the public relations group and the marketing group—particularly over the control of advertising that aims at reinforcing or modifying the company image.

The standard of living is a harmonic of the sales function in that it is the determinant of people's ability to pay for a product. The function of the sales group is to translate the ability to pay into a willingness to pay, and this is only possible if the ability is available.

In Figure 14 the two triangles are indicated differently. The government, technical associations, and public correspond to the structural dimension of a company, while the standard of living, raw materials, and technical knowledge correspond to the process dimensions of the company. The former manifest themselves through specific people whereas the latter are manifested through society at large. Some companies have employees or departments that look after some or all of these dimensions. Most companies have a lawyer as secretary of the company who provides the necessary expertise to deal with the legal and governmental problems. Most also have a purchasing agent concerned with getting raw materials, components, and equipment. Some companies have a person in charge of management development whose function is to tie in with universities and technical associations. Some companies also have a librarian whose function it is to maintain an up-to-date library of journals, technical papers, and books to provide adequate technical knowledge. Public relations managers are also often present, and frequently companies will employ an economist whose function is to monitor the changes in the level of the standard of living and changes in the mix of components making up a standard of living.

7. NOT TWO, NOT ONE

What is the difference between a dichotomy and a polarity? We have said that our approach to organization is bedeviled by dichotomies and yet we refer to polarities as an inevitable part of our existence. On the one hand we are seeking, in part, to show that a basic truth about a company is that it is a holon, i.e., that it has two centers— an "internal" center and an "external" one. On the other hand we have pointed out that the dichotomies of management come from a misunderstanding.

Dichotomies divide the world into either/or situations: something is either this or that. This either/or is built into our thinking framework; it is part of our logic. Aristotle formulated some basic patterns for thinking, and we in the West have been virtually ruled by these patterns ever since. These patterns were all based on an either/or standpoint.

Polarities do not divide the world, even though its two-ness is recognized. This is not to say that a polarity is a compromise. There are some people who are very dogmatic and who insist that everything is either right or wrong, good or bad. These people are often rightly cautioned to take into account the gradient between yes and no. There is a gradient scale of good and bad. However, this is not what is meant by a polarity. A famous illustration used by the Gestalt psychologists will help to explain the point:

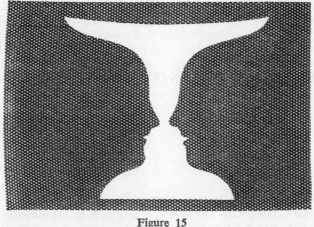

Figure 15

This illustration shows that the same phenomena can be interpreted in two quite distinct ways. There is a picture of two faces or a vase. Both are acceptable. We cannot say the picture is *either* two faces *or* a vase, nor can we say that it is both two faces and a vase because when it is two faces it is not a vase, and when it is a vase it is not two faces. We cannot "compromise" and have a gradient between the black of the two faces and the white of the vase. Either/or logic would either tear the picture in half or, at a more subtle level, cut around the outline of the faces: Both would destroy the situation.

In a similar way the phenomena of a company may be interpreted in two equally acceptable ways—for example, as structure or as process. The elements in both are the same, yet as long as one is considering structure, process will not be seen. As long as one is considering process, the structure will disappear.

A manager deals with dichotomies by thinking about them; he deals with polarities with a more fundamental part of himself, with what might be called his "intuition." Management science is based upon the assumption that a

manager is called upon to solve problems. What is being
suggested here is that although this is true, this is not the
whole story. A manager is also called upon to handle
polarities, and this is just where Zazen is of such value.

In addition to the structure/process polarity, the organization is pervaded by a number of others, all of which
have this baffling characteristic that one is figure and the
other is ground. The basic polarities are:

System	Individual
Urgent	Important
Cost	Quality
Waste	Risk
Process	Structure
Level	Span

The problem in a company is to balance the poles so
that each has its say, but neither predominates.

Structure/Process

With the structure/process polarity, the structural
functions are concerned with the important problems, the
most important of which is the continued survival of the
organization. The process functions, on the other hand, are
concerned with urgency, and the most urgent is getting
goods to the customer. If too much attention is given to
the structure of a company, it will make it top-heavy, cum-
bersome, and inert. Too much attention will likely be given
to details, and an increasing unwillingness to take risks will
result. On the other hand, too much attention to the
process function will create increasing amounts of waste
through false starts, lack of integration, and too much individual effort.

Peter Drucker has said that "each organization has the
task of balancing the need for order against the need for
flexibility and individual scope. Each requires a structure
determined by 'generic principles of organization,' that is,
in effect, by constitutional rules."[1] He goes on to ask
whether the structure should be absolute and according to

the principles of organization or whether it should be focused on specific objectives and strategy and by that means tailored to meet the logic of the situation. In other words, should it be tailored toward survival or toward self-assertion.

System/Individual

The system/individual polarity is encountered very frequently. The following is a familiar example: An employee requests time off with pay because her aunt has died. The personnel policy states that time off with pay is permitted when an immediate member of the family has died. The definition in the policy of "immediate family" does not include an aunt. The system, in this example, is represented by the personnel policy; the individual is represented by the employee requesting time off. On the face of it there is no problem. The answer is quite clear. The personnel policy does not allow a person to take time off with pay in order to mourn the death of an aunt. The system is clearly "figure," the individual clearly "ground."

However, the employee points out that her mother died when she was very young and the aunt has fulfilled the role of mother for her throughout her life. The personnel policy did not envisage such a relationship so there is a problem. If the manager accedes to the request, the system suffers; if the request is denied, the individual suffers. The system would suffer because if the employee is allowed time off with pay, the clarity of definition the policy once had would be diminished. The individual would suffer if not given time off because she will not be able to mourn the death of one she loved.

Urgent/Important

An interesting example of the urgent/important polarity occurred during World War II. Some, if not all, Spitfires were equipped with a special boosting device on the throttle. The pilot was able to increase the speed of the aircraft in an emergency by pushing the throttle through a "gate." If he did this, however, he increased the wear and tear on the aircraft considerably. The pilot was warned against using the booster for more than a specified time. If the booster were used for a longer period than specified, the vibrations could shake the engine off its mounting and the whole frame of the aircraft would be threatened. Thus, in combat the pilot was constantly faced with the polarity: urgent/important. Urgent: the enemy is bearing down with blazing guns! Important: the engine and the aircraft must be kept serviceable in order to get home and, where possible, fly again! In the urgent problem the time limits are known, the outcome uncertain, but the problem is obvious. With the important problem, on the other hand, the outcome is certain, the time unknown, and the problem hidden. Many people would say that the urgent problem is a practical one, whereas the important problem is a theoretical one. However, a crisis could be said to arise when the important problem becomes urgent. Most frequently urgent work takes precedence over important work. It is not surprising, therefore, that crises are precipitated in order to get important things done.

Cost/Quality

The cost/quality polarity is all too familiar. It is frequently expressed in the question, "How much quality do I sacrifice to save costs?" or, "How much do I increase my costs in order to have the extra quality that will give me the margin over my competitors?"

Waste/Risk

The waste/risk polarity is one that is less familiar to businessmen because they are more oriented toward one of the poles rather than both. Most businessmen recognize that they face the problem of risk in much of what they do, but strangely few recognize the problem of waste. Another way of stating this is that businessmen seem generally aware of the sin of commission but generally unaware of the sin of omission. The problem of waste and the burden created by it is one that is often carried unconsciously and is, therefore, the greater burden.

The waste/risk polarity can be understood very clearly by referring to the cycle of action that we have already shown to exist. A task cycle is made up of product development, product processing, and product-linking subcycles. There should be an appropriate balance between these three cycles. If this balance is reached, the waste/risk poles are also balanced. If inadequate product development is undertaken, then the risk is considerably increased. If, on the other hand, the product development phase is increased out of proportion to the other phase, then the likelihood of waste is increased.

An example of waste and risk occurs when someone undertakes a journey. To prepare adequately one must consult maps and be sure that the proposed route is the best available. It is quite possible that the time spent on consulting the map may be wasted; the road conditions may be such that the route selected turns out to be impossible. For this reason many people object to setting up plans, or, rather, undertaking product-development work. They say that no one can be sure that the situation will not have changed by the time the plan or project which has been developed is to be implemented.

Without consulting the map, however, one is constantly faced with the risk that the route one has taken will go through the most difficult terrain, or even in the wrong direction. Without a plan the situations that arise can only be dealt with on an *ad hoc* basis, and progress in the present may be bought at the expense of progress in the future.

The Japanese have a very keen sense of the product-development phase. Many Americans doing business with them feel that for some time the Japanese are simply wasting time. "To the Japanese the most important element in decision making is finding the question. The important and crucial steps are to decide whether there is a need for a decision and what the decision is about. . . . All of this takes a long time of course. The Westerner dealing with the Japanese is thoroughly frustrated during the process. He does not understand what is going on. He has the feeling that he is being given the run-around."[2]

8. CONFLICT AND GROWTH

We have said that the company can be looked upon as a six-dimensional force field; the forces representing its process, and the field representing its structure.[1] It has also been pointed out that the six-dimensional field is a field under tension. The forces are held together in dynamic equilibrium by the president, and he does this through the medium of the idea. The work of the company is to express this idea.

Thus, the forces within the field can be seen to be under tension in so far as they are at odds with each other. In so far as each of the positions may be delegated to separate managers, the situation is ripe for conflict, and conflict is what we experience within a company. Invariably there is conflict between the treasury, marketing, personnel, engineering, manufacturing, and sales functions within a company. Indeed, it is this very conflict that enables us to answer an important question. *If the framework provided by the univalent view is so unsatisfactory because it distorts the picture so badly, why is it so universally held and so vigorously defended?* Why is it that hard-nosed businessmen claim to be so altruistic that they will work for the welfare of shareholders whom they have never met and will never know, while at the same time affirm that business is no place for sentiment and idealism? Given that the field we have represented is correct, the answer will be obvious. This framework enables those managers to avoid facing up to conflict, and thus it enables them to reduce the level of work.

There is a tendency for the mind to simplify a problem and so solve it. But the simplifying approach that aims at reducing tension in the field is only of very limited value and can often stop a company from growing altogether. Sometimes it may even destroy it. As Chris Argyris says, "The American penchant for emphasizing happiness and pleasure overlooks the enormous part played by tension and discontent in achieving self-realization."[2] Generally we do not recognize conflict as part of the creative process that is necessary for any form of growth. The tendency is to suppress conflict, and from this suppression comes many of our psychological ills.

"Instead of trying to stamp out intergroup conflict as bad and disloyal, the executive must learn how to manage it so that the constructive aspects are emphasized and the destructive aspects de-emphasized."[3] The growth of an individual, as well as the growth of a company, arises from the struggle within himself to open himself fully to the creative potential of a situation and to express this potential through work. When he relies upon or is subjected to an inauthentic, facile solution, his growth, his creativity, and *his ability to do work* is reduced.

When conflict breaks out in a company it erupts as hostility, and the manager in whose department it occurs inevitably sees it as a conflict of personalities. There is only one form of conflict that is institutionalized and that is the labor/management conflict; all others are seen as originating from the personalities of individuals. For example, an article entitled "Coping with Organizational Conflict" stated that organizational problems and conflict develop "not because people are malicious (at least not often), but because varying life experiences have equipped all of us to see, feel, and appraise things more or less differently—inevitably producing conflict, stress, and often negative relationships."[4]

However, our studies will lead us to recognize that there are three forms of conflict, one of which is productive and two non-productive. Productive conflict comes from the nature of organization itself. Non-productive conflict arises either through poorly delegated work or through personality defects; the latter is probably much less frequent than managers would ever believe.

Given that each of the six functions—the three structure functions and the three process functions—is delegated to a separate manager, then productive conflict is possible. However, for a variety of reasons, some of which are perfectly valid, this pure delegation is rarely done. Consequently positions are split, and overlaps, duplications, omissions, and so on occur. These give rise to non-productive conflict. Because some conflict is desirable and other conflict is not, because the framework does not allow for desirable conflict, because managers have been trained to believe that all anxiety is neurotic, that human beings stop growing at about the age of sixteen, and because, in any case, the univalent view provides a simple either/or solution, the conflict is suppressed.

Instead of suppressing conflicts, specific channels could be created to make this conflict explicit, and specific methods could be set up by which the conflict is resolved. Out of this growth could arise. Unresolved conflict, on the other hand, will lead to frustration and hostility, and this in turn will tend to emphasize individual differences, personality defects, and, consequently, bring to the fore interpersonal hostility. Executives at the upper levels "tend to abhor open confrontation of conflict and emotions, and are almost completely unaware of ways in which to obtain genuine employee commitment to the organization. This results in upper-level systems in which there is a higher proportion of conforming, mistrust, antagonism, defensiveness, closedness, than of individuality, trust, concern and openness."[5] Managers who do not want to face up to the conflict inherent in work delegation, therefore exhort subordinates to "think of the well-being of the company as a whole" and insist that "we are all members of one great team and therefore should be willing to suppress our individual differences."[6] This is solving conflict in a non-creative way, in an old-man's way. Subordinates who insist upon attempting to realize the potential inherent in their position—they are invariably the most conscientious people with the greatest integrity—are frowned upon. They, in turn, become guilt-ridden because they cannot fit in and equally guilt-ridden because they are forced to stand by while valuable potential is lost.

The fear of conflict itself is one of the major causes of poor organization. Through refusing to face and reconcile conflict in a creative way, many managers subsume roles and tasks under departmental heads which should not functionally exist there. Sales and marketing are often found under the same heading, although they are obviously looking from two entirely different points of view at the same phenomena—the customer. The successful marketing manager has a different personality and temperament and, organizationally, a completely different outlook from the successful sales manager. By combining these two dimensions into one department, either the long-range strategy of the entire company is subjugated to immediate sales programs, or alternatively, sales programs are made impossibly difficult through a lack of concreteness and definiteness.

Engineering or product design is often subsumed under marketing in order to ensure that product development does not get "out of line" with the needs of the customer. Whereas marketing is concerned with the structural dimension, with how the resources of the company as a whole can be used, the engineering department is more concerned with the immediate task of realizing the potential of an existing product.

As we have said, in business there are two "sins": the sin of commission—doing what is done badly—and the sin of omission—not doing what needs to be done. The more conflict is suppressed, the greater the chances are that what is being done will be done with the minimum of disruption, argument, and delay; but on the other hand, the greater the chances are that more will be left out, more will be left undone. Trade-offs will be made that should never have been made, and this will in the end mean slower growth for the company. Fewer ideas will be generated, and the company will tend more and more to conform with what it has done in the past rather than develop new ways of doing things for the future.

We could envisage a company as a center and a surrounding field. The center is the point of maximum tension, and this tension is reduced as the periphery is approached. The greater the tension in the field, the higher the level of work necessary. The polarities we have discussed become more pressing as one ascends the hierarchy, and each of these polarities has its application along each of the six dimensions, which also become centralized in the person of the department heads and finally in the president. The tension also increases because as one ascends the hierarchy, longer time spans elapse between the perception of an idea and its realization as a product. This longer time span means that a manager is required to be able to operate within a wider "now" or present time than one who is operating at a lower level of time span. If one does *higher level* work, it does not mean that one does *more* work, or even *more important* work. To do higher level work means to express higher levels of tension through product-oriented perception and activity.

The concept of job enrichment that has been fairly popular in industry is based on this notion of differences in level of work. It has been recognized that the level of work given to an employee must offer some kind of challenge. Frequently, however, managers will give more work of the same, or even lower, level in the mistaken notion that job loading is the same as job enrichment. Job enrichment only occurs when the job gives increased challenge to the employee; that is, when it provides creative tension of a higher level.

This notion of level and its connection with conflict and tension shows up in another area—that of span of control. Although fewer people are paying the concept the attention that it once commanded, nevertheless it is important for us to consider some of its implications. The logic is that as a manager has "too many" subordinates answering to him, he appoints a manager between him and some or all of these subordinates, and thus has fewer direct subordinates. However, the employees reporting to this newly appointed manager will all experience a lowering of the level of work they are required to do. Tension inherent in the situation they were formerly expected to resolve now becomes the responsibility of the new manager, and the employees will experience a decrease in challenge. From this it would seem that there is an optimum number of levels within a company and that this number is related to the tension gradient in the field. This number is also likely to be fewer than the number frequently found in companies because organizing is often confused with dividing the spoils and managerial positions created as sinecures to give comfort to their incumbents rather than results to the company. A managerial role having task cycles requiring a time span of a year could comfortably have roles of four to six months reporting to it—not more, not less. If the roles do have more, unnecessary conflict is certain to occur; if less, then the manager will find that he is called upon to attend to detail of a level which is too low to maintain his interest.

This gives us a further opportunity to clarify the difference between growth and expansion. Growth is the capacity to take on higher level work; expansion is the ability for a given capacity to do more work. Growth is related to job enrichment, and expansion to job loading. Both companies and individuals can therefore grow. Given that a company is operating with an optimum number of levels of management, it will grow through the addition of a rank of management.

A rank-three company is one having three legitimate ranks of management, and it could grow to a rank four. The rank-three company has a lower level idea that it is expressing in its product than has a rank-four company. This means that the task cycle designed to produce the product will be longer in the case of the rank-four company than in the rank three. Specifically, this will mean that whereas the president of a rank-three company has a time span of two or three years, the president of a rank-

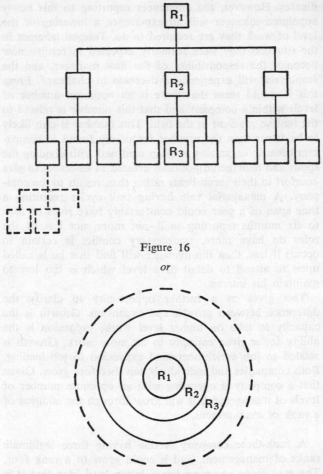

Figure 16

or

Figure 17

four company will have a time span of about five to seven years.[7] It will also mean that the company will require about six managers reporting to the president who have time spans of the level that the president had when the company was operating at optimum as a rank-three company. It will also require more finance, and so on. Growth in a company would in this way be growth along all dimensions, whereas expansion is simply growth along one. The usual view of the company organization chart is that it is a triangular-shaped structure (Figure 16). The view that we are suggesting is that it would be better regarded as a cone (Figure 17). The multidimensional field of the company is also a multileveled field, each level being called upon to resolve qualitatively different types of conflict.

9. STAFF AND LINE—THE BATTLE LINES OF BUSINESS

So far we have been looking at the company as a whole, and we have seen how this whole manifests itself along different dimensions or through different functions. The unit in which work is done is the role. But it has been stressed that the way in which roles fit together is of equal importance to the role's content in the understanding of organization. Unless role relationships are understood, the whole rhythm, harmony, and productive sequence of work is likely to be disrupted and roles will themselves degenerate. Indeed, this disruption is common throughout industry and is probably an important reason for the feeling of alienation and meaninglessness that so many people experience in industry. The obvious effects of this breakdown include time wastage, extreme frustration, and poor performance. But more important than these even is the hidden effect; the failure of organizations to grow as they should.

Conflict and tension are not necessarily undesirable. Conflict arising out of the polarities inherent in an organization is desirable. However, conflict arising through poor timing, frustration, and system breakdown is undesirable; indeed it is pathological and should not be tolerated. Yet most organizations actively foster this degenerative conflict through an organization approach called *staff and line*. A study of staff/line theory will help to illustrate this condition.

The staff/line theory says that some members of a company make decisions while others give advice. This staff/line approach was adopted from the military organization, and it is widespread throughout industry. "Almost every business of any consequence at all in the United States today is a corporation with the line-and-staff pattern of organization."[1]

The logic of the staff and line is simple. The proponents of the approach say, or imply, the following: Someone must make a decision. Conflict is endemic to an organization, and this conflict arises out of the natural contentiousness of people. Therefore, to be able to make decisions we must reduce the area of contention to a minimum, and we can do this in two ways. The first is by ensuring that each man has but one boss. This boss, furthermore, must have undisputed power over the subordinate and can therefore force him, by threat of dismissal and loss of his livelihood and self-esteem, to toe the line. The second is by dividing the company into two divisions; the conflict area is thereby reduced, and conflict can be resolved by the simple expedient of asking who in this situation is staff and who is line?

This logic worked well in the seventeenth century when the concept was first introduced to a military organization by Gustavus Adolphus. Power is the raw material that is used by the military machine, and the principal problem was how to contain and direct this power. An army is a holon, as is any other living system, but it is a holon in which the survival/expression dilemma, when it is seriously posed, is solved in favor of survival. The basic problem confronting an army is how to survive in situations that threaten it with disintegration and destruction. The threat, moreover, comes from within the holon, through panic, as well as from the outside, through an overwhelming force being applied by an opposing army. Individual initiative is not needed—"theirs is not to reason why"—and frustration simply generates the type of power most prized and needed in combat.

Early industrial organizations, lacking any discipline or structure of their own, working within a context of competition, and furthermore being dominated by an entrepreneurial univalent framework, would naturally adopt the organization of the most successful institutions. The army was therefore an appropriate model. However, because of a fundamental shift from entrepreneurial to professional management and of the shift from control through coercion to control through influence, the basic context has changed and the staff/line approach is no longer acceptable.

"There is probably no other single area of management which in practice causes more difficulties, more friction and more loss of time and effectiveness."[2] "Line and staff may well be the cause of much of the administration confusion from which many companies suffer."[3] "No other two words are more frequently misunderstood and misused in ordinary business parlance. When the subject comes up in some companies a long argument ensues and eventually it is politely decided that the whole subject is rather more theoretical than practical and that no real reason to make the distinction exists."[4]

The American Management Association conducted a survey of company organization. The research was based upon questionnaires completed by 118 American companies, among which were some of the largest organizations in the United States. In his comments, the author, K. K. White, illustrates (albeit unwillingly) the confusion of the average businessman about the meaning and place of staff/line in organization. This confusion is demonstrated by self-contradiction, by a subtle shift in the definition of terms, and so on. We shall, therefore, make a critical review of White's essay as this could be looked upon as representative of the North American businessman. White sampled the thoughts of businessmen and drew upon these samples in writing his essay.

The fundamental confusion in the staff/line concept is to be found in the word "line." This word has two quite different meanings. In the first place, White says, staff/line units have come into being because of rank within an organization. "If those of a higher rank were to give orders to all at a lower rank, business would become unmanageable, and therefore staff/line came into being. Therefore, in human organizations, no one can give direct

orders to another unless he is a direct *line* superior, and
this is true regardless of rank 'or at least it should hold
true.' "[5]

He then goes on to give another, different definition: "A
line activity is that activity for which the organization was
created."[6] It is that main on-going activity without which
the company would cease to exist. For example, "The
main purpose of an army is to fight, and anyone whose
chief duty is to fulfill this purpose is in the line. As the accounting department has no part in the physical construction of the company's product, it must be staff."[7]

Thus, there are two meanings to the word "line." The
first meaning is associated with what we have referred to
as the survival mode, and the second with the expansive
mode of the organization's activity. The function of the
first type of line activity is to ensure company survival by
its remaining integrated. This involves the whole company
and, as we have seen, can be done in a creative way by
providing the means for expressing conflict inherent within
organization; or it can be done by eliminating one or other
parties in the conflict. In either case, it concerns the organization-as-structure.

The second kind of line activity is qualitatively different
from the first. It occurs in a different dimension and concerns *organization-as-process*. It concerns the organization
in its expansive mode. This again involves the whole company.

The very term "line" is, therefore, ambiguous and as its
ambiguity rests upon the basic polarities of a company and
as polarities "can neither be broken into two parts nor its
contradiction resolved,"[8] there can be no wonder that the
line and staff problem causes so much distress.

White says that the identification of line activity is sometimes difficult, and frequently mistakes are made. However, the differentiation between line and staff must be
done "and the whole kernel for this differentiation" lies in
preventing a member of the staff personnel from "trying to
arrogate to himself the power of determining the success
or failure of the line units."[9]

In this statement we see the real value of the staff/line theory is that it drives conflict underground, and so conflict ceases to be a recognizable problem for a manager.

However, this "solution" is arrived at on the one hand by a term that veils the very creative source of a company —its primary polarity—and on the other hand by using a term that destroys any hope of understanding what work is and any hope of delegating it properly. In other words, the staff/line theory is a theory which by itself causes degeneration, and a company's success occurs in spite of and not because of this theory.

The problem is not that the staff/line theory recognizes two dimensions; the problem is that it *only* recognizes two dimensions. There is no freedom in the theory to pass from the two dimensions to the whole.

What is in question in challenging the staff/line theory is not whether there are two dimensions to a situation: a "staff" dimension (an advisory, perceptual, theoretical, structural dimension) and a "line" dimension (an active, pragmatic, process dimension). What is in question is whether these dimensions can always be fixed and institutionalized within specific and invariable role structures.

One of the most common statements in industry is that "staff" departments do not make decisions. This is not true, and to maintain this belief is to disregard a great many obvious facts. A salary administrator decides what sort of salary administration system to introduce, including methods of job analysis, job evaluation, methods for setting grades, methods for keeping grades up to date, when and how salary reviews will be conducted, and many other such decisions. The labor relations manager decides on contract interpretation, how to handle grievances, when to take a case to arbitration, contract strategy, and so on. And yet K. K. White says that the personnel function is almost invariably regarded as a staff specialization no matter what the main activity of the company may be.[10]

Indeed, he says, "Here we find perhaps the clearest representation of what a pure staff department or executive should be. This is because every manager is obliged to practice the art of personnel administration and the personnel manager came into being when the line managers realized that there is simply too much work to be done or that they are in need of competent assistance. All other staff specializations are born and develop out of similar needs."[11]

Yet the work of the finance department does not arise because there is "simply too much work to be done" or because a manager is "in need of competent advice and assistance." The work of the finance department arises because of the need to raise finances and to explain to investors how their money has been used and what profit they have derived as a consequence of their investments. It might be said that the manufacturing manager, if he did not have so much work to do and therefore had more time available, could obtain his own finance or do his own marketing. But it could equally well be said that if the treasurer did not have so much work to do, he could do his own manufacturing. Indeed, such an argument misses the whole point of organization.

The director of the manpower management division of the United States Department of the Navy in Washington, Ambrose Klotz, wrote a critical review of the staff/line theory and said that the traditional view is out of date in the contemporary world. He points out that "in articles emphasizing the traditional and exclusive line function of decision-making, the repeated message is that the decision *should* be made by line officials. The unspoken implication is one of protestation that frequently staff officials do exercise decision authority."[12]

Klotz says that the "nebulous distinctions regarding the degree of directness of contribution toward mission accomplishment is no longer a useful criterion for distinguishing line from staff, assuming that such a distinction need be made at all."

Some might argue that although the theory may not be elegant, nevertheless the staff/line approach is a workable arrangement and is justified in practice. It will later be shown that the assumption that it can be a practical mode of behavior is without any psychological foundation. Indeed it will be shown to be in direct opposition to the deepest psychological needs of men. For the moment, it will be sufficient to show that the theory does not work in practice.

As early as 1950, Melville Dalton, in a paper "Conflicts Between Staff and Line," pointed out the main practical consequences of the staff/line theory. He said this "structure of specialized experts advising busy administrators has in a number of significant cases failed to function as expected. The assumptions that (1) the staff specialist would be reasonably content to function without a measure of formal authority over production, and that (2) their suggestions regarding improvement of processes and techniques for control over personnel and production would be welcomed by line officers and be applied require closer examination. In practice, there is often much conflict between industrial staff and line organizations, and in varying degrees the members of these organizations oppose each other."[13] He says later in the paper that this conflict involved all members of management, especially those in the middle and lower ranks. *"The intensity of the conflict was aggravated by the fact that it was formally unacceptable and had to be hidden"* (author's italics). Theoretically it was felt that the staff/line concept should work.

One of the more interesting consequences of the conflict between staff and line personnel is the development of alliances and collusions between staff and line people. According to Dalton, "staff personnel, particularly in the middle and lower levels, carried on expedient relations with the line that daily evaded formal rules. Even those officers most devoted to rules found that, in order not to arouse enmity in the line on a sufficient scale to be communicated *up* the line, compromising devices were frequently helpful and sometimes almost unavoidable both for organizational and career aims."[14]

Thus it would be true to say that the staff/line theory is not complete, in that to be presented at all it must ignore the fact that "staff personnel" make decisions with as much authority and as directly as do "line personnel." It is furthermore not workable, as the quotations that we have given from various authors show. It is not communicable as it fails to define one of its key terms, "line," in an unambiguous way. It is claimed that the system is simple. However, this simplicity is derived from an either/or logic which deals only in discrete atomic elements, and a system must be fragmented to be understood and dealt with according to this logic. Furthermore, the staff/line theory begs a very important issue, and it is in this that its principal failure is to be found: What is the accountability of staff personnel? Staff personnel are thought to be responsible for the quality of the advice they give, but as Dalton points out, they are invariably held responsible only for whether or not this advice is accepted.

10. THREE STRUCTURAL FUNCTIONS

A role and a company are isomorphic. A role is a whole, a monad, with boundaries and a core represented by its purpose or product. It will be seen that a role is a holon, having an integrative and assertive mode. It also will find expression through the triad of resources, skills, and needs, and this expression will be found to give rise to a structure and process having six dimensions.

Each role has one or more products by which it can be identified. Through this product, therefore, the role can be linked to the wider environment, which is the company. A company has the requirement to "sell" its product, and a role has a similar requirement. It might be better in most cases to use a "soft sell" approach. This soft sell might be of the nature of giving advice rather than giving orders. But this is a mode of behavior within a role rather than a characteristic of the role itself.

The key to understanding role differences is in the different *products* they produce and not in the different *structures* they have, because such a difference does not exist. Instead of there being two fundamentally different role structures in a company, all roles have the same structure, but the product of each differs. A few of the products are directly related to the company environment. The majority of them, however, act as inputs, limits, or control devices on the products of others. A company is "fully interlocking," and this effect is achieved through the products of the roles, each role having its inherent authority. As Drucker said, "Unless each recognizes the authority inherent in the 'logic of the situation' and the knowledge of individuals, there will be no performance. Unless each also has a decision-making authority beyond which there is no appeal, there will be no decisions."[1]

Some of the products are concerned primarily with giving expression to the process or self-assertive dimension of the company. Other products are concerned with the structural or survival dimension of the company. However, it is very important to realize that one cannot substitute "staff" for "structure" and "line" for "process." This would be tantamount to saying that a company could express itself in an assertive mode without survival, or that a company could survive without some contribution being made to society.

All roles produce one or more products. A role that does not produce a product is an incomplete role and will act as a parasite on the organization. The first step in writing a role description must be to determine the product or products of that role—the result expected from it. All of the products from all of the roles are coalesced within the total system of an expanding, self-regulating, or growing company. The products from roles within the structural dimension maintain the viability of the organization's structure. They enable the company to remain integrated. The products of roles within the process dimension are coalesced in the product sold by the company. They are the products that enable the company to acquire self-assertiveness.

The staff/line theory is based on an understanding of work in behavior terms, not in product terms. Work and activity are not differentiated. If the product, purpose, or goal of a role is not defined, it will be assumed that people are expected to go through motions, such as "checking budgets," "filling in forms," or "turning on valves" and that this constitutes work. In such circumstances it is possible for activities such as advising and assisting to take on the appearance of work when, in fact, they are ways in which work is done.

Each role must have the full responsibility, authority, and accountability required to produce a product. A product is an idea in a form with a demand. Responsibility relates to seeing what needs to be done. It is related to the *idea*. Authority is related to committing resources in order that what is seen as needing to be done can be done. It is related to the *form*. Accountability arises through demonstrating that what has been produced meshes with the requirements of the total system. It, in turn, is related to the *demand*. Just as a product cannot be reduced to a distinct idea, a distinct form, and a distinct demand, each separate from the other, so it is not possible to separate responsibility, authority, and accountability within a role.

In each role market research is necessary. Each role occupant must identify his market and determine the needs of that market. This market research may be looked upon as obtaining the advice and assistance of others within the field. Each role, furthermore, must have the means for mobilizing and committing resources required to produce the product, and each role must be able to demonstrate that the product which has been created fits into the requirements of the total system.

A company is in business to "realize" the potential of an idea by giving it a form through which it can be linked within the environment. This realization must be done in such a way that the environment is prepared to work to have that idea in that form. Furthermore, this realization takes place in the field that is made up of employees, shareholders, and customers. The product idea, because it has different dimensions, therefore causes different aspects of the company to assume the center of focus at different times. The center of gravity is constantly changing, and to attempt to fix that center by saying that one function is *the* important company function causes an artificial crystallization in the company so that it is no longer freely adaptable to the changing circumstances in which it finds itself. The essence of an organization is the expression of change. As circumstances change, so does the center of gravity and so does the "line function" of the company.

Growth is "self-regulated expansion" along all dimensions. As long as the center of gravity can move freely between all dimensions in the company, growth becomes possible. But if the center of gravity is fixed in one or two dimensions, then expansion alone can occur, and this gives rise to the cataclysmic approach to organization in which periodically a total shift is necessary from the process dimension to the structural dimension. These cataclysmic changes, of course, are very damaging to the constitution of the company and also cause considerable suffering among its personnel.

The three "structural" functions that were shown to exist need some explanation because often these are the ones about which there is the most confusion. This confusion arises out of the failure to recognize structure as something in its own right. Behaviorists have either deliberately ignored or even attempted to refute the reality of structure, and as behaviorism is most often taught, managers are inclined more to behaviorism than to other psychologies that are more structurally oriented. If the role and importance of structure as a primordial condition of being is ignored or denigrated, then those functions within a company concerned with structure are likewise likely to suffer the same fate. The result of this would be to relegate these functions to "staff" status and then deny that these staff functions have any effective role to play by changing their decision making into "advice" and "assistance." This would cause a serious break to occur in the company organization. Let us consider some of the confusion surrounding the three structural departments.

The marketing function is concerned with anticipating the future. It is not product development, but together with product development it creates the future. Neither is marketing planning. The word "planning" is a much-abused word and is used interchangeably for both product development and marketing.

A market is a set of needs that can be satisfied by the work of a company. These needs are among an ocean of needs, some of which are clearly known and fully articulate, some of which are vague and ill-expressed, while others are still unconscious and waiting to surface. Like water in the ocean, needs are in constant flux, some rising to the surface, others subsiding, some expanding, others contracting.

The marketing function is, therefore, to perceive the need and to determine alternative ways for satisfying that need at a profit. The more needs that the marketing function can perceive and the greater the number of ways that are available to the company for satisfying that need, the greater the company's potential. In addition, the marketing function is to make needs *articulate*. An articulate need is one for which there is a willingness to pay to have the need satisfied. The impetus to its becoming articulate is often given through advertising and sales promotion. There is a scale or hierarchy of needs that is related to this articulateness, and the marketing function is to raise a set of needs up this hierarchy.

The market need therefore makes the product cycle of action possible. Marketing must be distinguished quite clearly from the selling function, which comes at the end of the cycle. Selling and service, what we have called product linking, is concerned with the customer as an individual. The market is a set of needs with the willingness to pay to have the need satisfied. The customer is that need with the willingness to pay and *with the ability to pay*. A salesman must translate need into demand. It is not enough that a salesman identifies that a specific customer has a specific need. He must also translate that need into a demand by arousing the willingness to pay to have that need satisfied. The market is a structure. Demand is the market in action; it is process. From the results of the marketing function the company is able to set up an adequate financial structure to meet the future needs of the changing opportunities. It can also set up the recruiting, training and development, and organizing necessary to have a satisfactory staff. It can assess and give significance to its selling activity and provide the groundwork for new product development or improved design. The company can do this because of the future created by the marketing department. On the skill and insight of the marketing department depends the company's ability to have parallel cycles of action. The more one can anticipate the future, the more certainly can one undertake action designed to cope with the needs of the future. With a good marketing department, improved delegation is possible.

The function of human resources mobilization is concerned with mobilizing, organizing, and motivating employees. It is most often known as a department by the name of personnel or industrial relations. Organizing, manning, and motivating should form the basis of the personnel department. Just as the marketing department has the function of structuring the needs of the market so that the product cycle can be linked through the willingness and ability of customers to pay, so the personnel department has the function of structuring the employees in such a way that the product cycle may be undertaken.

Some of the problems encountered in industry can be explored in this light. Traditionally a manager's function has been to plan, *organize,* and control. Each manager, therefore, has the responsibility to organize. How can it therefore be said that the personnel function is to organize? A manager is required to organize along the process dimension: He must organize to get the product out. Each department has one or more products, and therefore each has product cycles. The personnel department has the function to clarify the organization limits. The personnel department *organizes to enable organization-as-process to occur.* The personnel function is concerned with the interfaces between departments; it ensures that these interfaces do not clash. Given that a company is a system of roles that are independent but mutually related, the personnel function is concerned with the relationship between roles.

Because in industry the distinction between the two types of organization—organization-as-structure and organization-as-process—has not been made clear, the personnel department has been frequently frustrated in its function and has tended to crystallize around another function: the function of labor relations. This has two serious consequences. The first is that the company does not have an organization-as-structure, and it therefore operates like a badly timed car. The second is that the human resources department undertakes a task that causes it to perpetuate rather than resolve the labor/management dichotomy, a dichotomy that is costing our society so much. This task is the labor relations task and by undertaking this as its central occupation, the personnel department destroys completely its chance of doing the work that the organization really requires it to do.

Labor relations is not a function that a company performs on its own behalf, but one that it performs on behalf of society. An industry performs several of these functions on behalf of society, including tax collecting and providing welfare services such as pensions, disability insurance, and so on. Some companies go further and provide educational services and even hospital and other medical services. These are not activities related to the industrial economic enterprise. This is not to say that they should not be done by that enterprise; on the contrary, as the industrial enterprise benefits from such services and as the expertise of the enterprise lends itself to this sort of work being done well, then it is desirable that they should be done by a company. However, because work is done *by* a company, that work is not therefore necessarily *of* the company.

An example may help to clarify this point. Some managers find that they are called upon to act on various committees outside the company, and they are asked to do this work because the work they normally do makes them particularly suited to help the committee fulfill its function. This function may have a distinct bearing upon the work of the manager, and the committee's decisions, if they are wise, may help him to do his own work more easily. But even so, this committee work is not the work of the company. Thus, work is done *by* a manager, but it is not work *of* that manager.

Another example will help to justify the contention that labor relations work is not work of a company. Earth tremors sometimes occur on the Reef in the Transvaal in

South Africa when disused mines subside. These earth tremors cause faults to appear in the terrain. Architects who build on this terrain must take the faults into account when designing buildings. In other parts of the world this is not necessary. Therefore, it can be said that taking the quality of the terrain into account is part of the function of an architect, but taking into account fissures likely to arise due to rock falls in disused mines is a particular and local problem imposed on an architect. It is not inherently his function, but nonetheless must be resolved by him.

These examples now allow us to address the labor relations problem which could be likened to a fault in the social terrain. While labor relations are important and must be taken into account, what should be recognized is that whereas organization and manning is an intrinsic part of the structural part of the company, labor relations is not.

The damage caused by this confusion is not confined simply to misplaced and inappropriate expertise. The social fissure of which labor relations is an outcome is a function of the attitude toward property ownership and is derived from an earlier world outlook. The social fissure comes from the dichotomy of owner/employee, of which modern industry still feels it is the faithful champion. In other words, the labor/management conflict arises through a failure on the part of both sides to recognize that managers are not owners, but employees. This failure is to the detriment of both.

Because of the confusion that exists in the mind of the personnel manager about his role, he neglects the organizing function in which he would be concerned with enhancing the potentiality inherent in the employees and assumes instead another function. The personnel manager then sees his basic function as a bargaining agent on behalf of the shareholder. It is not surprising to find, in companies not large enough to have independent personnel departments, that the personnel function is performed by the treasurer or by someone answering to him.

In this situation where the true function is neglected by

the personnel department, the function will be taken over in a debased way by unions. The word debased is used not as a reflection upon unions, which have a perfectly legitimate social role to play, but because the union role is a *social* one and not a management role. An enlightened union will take over the responsibility of ensuring that the potential of the employees is not wasted.

To an increasing extent, professional and white-collar employees are joining associations. This is not due simply to dissatisfaction with pay, but because of a general sense of dissatisfaction that talents and abilities are being wasted. It is quite likely that much of the conflict over "management rights" that occurs in labor relations occurs because personnel managers are unable to carry out the function of organizing so that organization can take place.

In carrying out its organizing function the personnel department must also ensure that there is sufficient human capacity to make that organization work. Each manager must ensure that he has sufficient staff of sufficiently high capacity to be able to carry out the work of his department. However, in a viable management development program, managers should be given thorough experience of the company which will entail promotion across departmental boundaries. Sufficient staff must also be recruited in order to take care of attrition and future growth. A further function of the personnel department is to set up a structure to enable employees to be paid fairly. Once more managers of employees have specific responsibilities in determining the "merit" of each employee and ensuring that he is paid according to this merit.

It can therefore be seen that both the personnel department and the managers of the other departments have specific responsibilities and appropriate task cycles. However, these task cycles are in different dimensions; they are in different time frames. By recognizing that there are a set of cycles that are the legitimate cycles of the personnel group, this department could carry out these cycles and so relieve other managers of work. However, this should be done on a basis of equality with the other departments.

The last function that we wish to review is the finance function. This function is concerned with mobilizing, structuring (through budgets), and accounting for finance. It is concerned with realizing the potential that the company has to acquire financial investment and to make this money available at the required points within the company. There is confusion about the finance function, and it will be worthwhile commenting upon this confusion. It arises partly from a semantic confusion about the word "profit," partly from the numinous quality of money and its symbolic significance, and partly from the fact that the structure of the company is as important as the process of a company.

Profit may have a narrow meaning—the excess of income or the money retained by the owner after he has paid his operating expenses—or a wider, systems-oriented connotation. Galbraith noted the oddity of professional managers maintaining that they are working hard—sometimes up to twelve or more hours a day—so that the "owners" can get more money. Feedback in a system represents stability and serves the integrating function of the system. Just as there are three inputs—need, know-how, and finance—there are three feedbacks: reinvested finance, increased know-how, and increased good will which increases the willingness to pay to have the company's product. These three feedbacks are all profit in a larger meaning of that word, and it is in this context that professional managers should operate.

But the confusion about the finance function is deeper than a mere semantic confusion about the word profit. The confusion stems from the significance of money. Money is the means by which decisions are made effective. It is like a "carrier wave" of decisions. Decisions are acts of will, and money transmutes individual decisions into social decisions, thereby magnifying that decision. The social value of money is that it enables complex systems to be linked both internally and between themselves. Within a company the roles and departments are linked by decisions, but the link is made possible by money. Budgets are the structural aspect of the finance function.

Money, as we know too well, not only has a social value, but also a value to people who control it. It magnifies decisions, but because of this, because it gives individuals social power, it comes to have a value that is now anti-social and becomes a disruptive force. The inner-togetherness of groups that money is designed to promote is disrupted through the urge to possess it. Will, as we have said, is the *urge* to self-realization; money is a direct expression of this will because money allows society to realize itself. People therefore seek to find a short cut to self-realization through money. However, when money is diverted from its social role to serving individuals it becomes as destructive as formerly it was liberating, because it increases the autonomy of the elements at the cost of the mutual relatedness of those elements within the system.

Money also has the function of a measure of value, which derives from its linking function. Just as the man who is at the center of the communication lines of a group will acquire control and prestige in that group, the man who is at the center of the flow of finance will, for similar reasons, acquire prestige. The man, or company, who can command the greatest finance, commands the greatest prestige because it is inferred that he has the greatest value.

The finance function consists of realizing the potential to command money, enabling this money to be used through budgets to enhance the structure of the company, and to keep the scorecard. Budgets are structured finance and should be designed to enable departments and roles within departments to make effective decisions. Each responsibility should be backed by an appropriate authority —this is a fundamental article in the managerial credo. Budgets are the means by which the finance department is able to determine what finance is required in the future. They are also the means by which this finance enters the structure of the company. Accounts, on the other hand, are the means by which the scorecard is kept. The monthly statements and the year-end report are the basic means by which companies let others know whether they are winning or losing. Unfortunately, budgets are often operated as though they were a part of the accounting process. They are allocated in such a way that the accounting department has the minimum difficulty in determining which account should be charged with a particular expenditure. It is then presumed that budgets, like accounts, should balance. So instead of following the *decision structure,* instead of money being available at *decision points,* budgets follow the *accounting structure* which may be, and often is, at odds with the decision structure.

The consequence of this is very serious. The relationship between roles can be maintained only by a correct interaction between decision points. Because the budget—and therefore the flow of money—follows the accounting structure and not the decision structure, it will inevitably follow that there will be money distributed to managers who do not legitimately have decisions to make; and managers who do have decisions to make will not get the money. Such budgets will therefore enhance the potential of individuals and not of roles. The finances of the company will be used to make individuals powerful rather than to give roles the authority that is needed for tasks to be accomplished. Authority could be looked upon as institutionalized power, or power expressed through roles that are defined in part by decision points.

Thus, much of the confusion in the relationship between roles is created by the overriding accounting orientation. The confusion is perpetuated by its very success—the success in giving power to individuals and not roles—because the individuals who get such power have a vested interest in perpetuating that very confusion. The confusion is increased because there will not be enough money available at points where decisions should be made, which will cause time lags, frustration, and frequently poor-quality work.

11. TYPES OF WORK

Many of the difficulties that managers experience when talking about work come from the poverty of our language. Not only is it inadequate because the word "work" is not properly defined, it is also inadequate because we have but one word to designate what is in fact a very complex field. This leads us to look upon work as just one type of activity, and because we do this, we lead ourselves into endless problems. Work has a common structure. This common structure is given in its definition and is common to all types of work. But there are a number of different kinds of work.

Edmund Carpenter, commenting upon the language of the Eskimo, pointed out that because snow is so important to the Eskimo, there are many words to describe it. His comments are worth repeating as what he has to say points up the importance of the adequacy of words. "Language is the principal tool with which the Eskimos make the natural world a human world. They use many words for snow which permit fine distinctions, not simply because they are much concerned with snow, but because snow takes its form from the actions in which it participates: sledging, falling, igloo building, blowing. These distinctions are possible only when experienced in a meaningful context. Different kinds of snow are brought into existence by the Eskimos as they experience their environment and speak. The words do not label something already there."[1] Just as different kinds of snow have been brought into existence by the Eskimo as they experience their environment and talk about it, so different kinds of work can be brought into the industrial West. Nine different types of work can be distinguished: three of these concern the type of commitment, and six concern the process of doing work. Because we have not defined these our experience is that much poorer, and our activity to that extent the more unreliable.

Commitment

The three types of work relating to commitment are "employment," "entrepreneurial," and "intrinsic interest" work.

Employment work is that which is done for pay and the limits of which are prescribed by the manager of the role. It is the work that enables the company to survive and expand. If employment work is not done, a company cannot go on. The need for the product of employment work is specified by the role manager, and it is also the role manager's responsibility to ensure that the product idea is capable of satisfying that need. In employment work a manager must delegate or make known all three limits, and these limits are therefore adjusted to each other. The subordinate's responsibility is to ensure that the maximum potential within these limits is realized. He must therefore find as many different ways of expressing the product idea as possible. The product is therefore variable within limits.

Most of us are familiar with the notion of the entrepreneur. He is responsible for identifying new needs and perceiving new ways in which these needs can be satisfied. It is he who sets up new markets and new product ideas. The entrepreneur, because he does something new and untried, takes a risk that is not taken by someone who simply does employment work. The person doing employment work can be shown to be wrong because his work does not meet required standards. Likewise, the entrepreneur can be shown to be wrong if he happens to commit himself to the wrong idea.

Entrepreneurial work can be done by an employee of a company within the context of that company. To do this, he must identify a need that hitherto has not been recognized by the company, perceive a product idea that will satisfy that need, generate a demand for the product, and create the product. When he does this an employee is no longer doing employment work because he has moved out of the limits imposed by his manager. Furthermore, his manager *qua* manager can no longer sanction his action. To the extent that a man is doing entrepreneurial work, he is without a manager, he is a stranger and exposed to the risks of a stranger.

If the product idea is of a sufficiently high level, its realization could require a considerable realignment of the company. Therefore, higher levels of management must be persuaded to adopt the idea, and the risk increases at higher levels. Strangers have always been subject to threat and persecution, and the entrepreneur within industry may suffer likewise. To fill the role, a man must "stick his neck out." As he must also fill the needs of his employment work, he must either be capable of organizing that work well so that he has spare time to pursue entrepreneurial work, or he must do this latter work in his spare time.

Many companies recognize the need for entrepreneurial work and have tried to encourage employees to undertake it through suggestion boxes. Suggestion boxes, however, invariably fail because entrepreneurial work requires commitment different than that of employment work. "New ideas" are not enough; one must be willing to expose oneself to a potentially hostile environment. A man who is prepared to risk his reputation, who is willing to invest time and energy in the realization of an idea, and who in any case has the creativity necessary to perceive the idea is highly committed to ensuring that the idea is introduced. It is this sort of commitment that enables a man to grow, to realize his potential in a new way.

Entrepreneurial work, therefore, is that work which sets up new patterns and new possibilities because it generates a new need, whereas employment work satisfies an already existing need.

There is another kind of work for which it is not necessary to generate a need because the need already exists, but it is not employment work because one does not get paid for doing it. It is work done because it is intrinsically interesting; it is its own reward. Work done in service clubs, the Jaycees, church work, charitable work, or work promoting junior sports, are examples of intrinsic-interest work.

Intrinsic-interest work is also done in a company. One very important kind of intrinsic-interest work is that done when assisting and advising others. Each role must have its own reason for being. Each role serves a specific need of the organization as a whole. Once this is recognized, then "advice" and "assistance" are something given outside the range of employment work.

The words "advise," "assist," and "collaborate with" are often used to describe task cycles within employment work. This creates confusion because managers are thereby forced to give "advice" to others, and others are forced to take it or at least give the impression of taking it. Advice, however, is only such provided that it can be freely accepted or rejected. Therefore, advice is something that can only be sought; it cannot be imposed. Advice comes from the Latin *ad videre*, "to see." To produce a product it is necessary to "perceive" the idea. The one who perceives the idea is the one who produces the product. If roles are linked according to products, this will not create a problem. If, however, roles are linked according to advice, then a conflict is inevitable as the two will likely perceive different product ideas within the same field.

If a manager is paid to give his advice to others, he will necessarily do everything he can to get others to accept it. If others refuse the advice, then the one called upon to give it will feel that his livelihood is threatened, and to an increasing degree he will come to concentrate upon selling himself and tailoring his advice to meet his client, rather than to meeting the needs of the situation.

However, the adviser may have friends in high places, and he is thereby able to force his advice on others. Those who are put into the position of having to receive advice resent it. They resist receiving it and avoid calling for it.

Sometimes they may need advice; sometimes they may need someone to talk to, someone to confide in. But they hesitate to call for advice as they know from previous experience that they are simply calling for someone to take over the very work they are paid to do. Therefore, they also feel their livelihood is threatened.

The effect of this is, of course, to bring about a breakdown in communications. Roles develop shells around themselves, and intrinsic-interest work withers. This, in turn, brings about a disintegration of the company structure and, therefore, an increase in the need to use power to hold the company together. More senior levels of management threaten overtly or covertly those who are defending their right to work, and so increase the tendency toward withdrawal and increased disintegration.

By definition, one is not paid for doing intrinsic-interest work: It is its own reward, and people will want to do it for its own sake. Therefore, a company that is well organized, in which employees are secure in their employment work, would also have employees willing to advise and assist others, as well as employees willing to seek advice from others. It would, therefore, be a well-integrated company and would suffer relatively few communication problems. Furthermore, the more intrinsic-interest work that is done, the more interesting the company is and the more enjoyable it becomes.

The confusion created by using one word to speak about three quite different ways of behaving will mean that poor decisions will be made. For example, employment work is paid for by salaries, and this work should be the basis upon which salary structures and salary increases are made. However, salary increases are often given for entrepreneurial work and even more frequently for intrinsic-interest work. Entrepreneurial work should be paid for in the long run by promotion. A man who is capable of entrepreneurial work is frequently capable of being promoted. In the short run, it should be paid for by a bonus. Intrinsic-interest work should not be paid for in salaries because if it is, it becomes employment work with the consequences described above. However, the astute administrator will not ignore the fact that an employee performs this kind of work because, like all other work, it is best done in the light of recognition. But the administrator will not commit the blunder of "merit" rating an employee on "co-operation," "loyalty," etc. Co-operativeness and loyalty, intrinsic-interest work in fact, cannot be bought, but this is no reason for it not being rewarded.

Entrepreneurial work causes conflict. It must do so. Managers move out of their role structure and move into the role structure of others. People resent strangers, and this work is therefore a threat to the integration of a company.

In a company that has too many entrepreneurs there will be considerable conflict. Entrepreneurs rock the boat and they also rock one another. Poorly organized companies cannot tolerate this conflict and suppress the entrepreneur. If, however, the manager of an entrepreneur recognizes that entrepreneurial work is different from employment work, that it does mean crossing boundaries, that it does mean innovation and change and all that change implies, then he will diagnose the conflict correctly and instead of looking for ways to suppress the conflict and punish the person responsible for causing it, he will seek to find ways of giving that conflict constructive channels of expression, channels that enable the potential in the situation to be realized.

The very basis of a company structure is therefore well-organized employment work because this generates the willingness to engage in intrinsic-interest work, which, in turn, creates a climate for entrepreneurial work. Entrepreneurial work and intrinsic-interest work are opposites reconciled by employment work. Intrinsic-interest work enables the company to acquire a natural self-regulation, while entrepreneurial work enables the company to expand naturally. Employment work that includes integration as well as expansion enables the company to grow. Entrepreneurial work enables new patterns, new possibilities, to come into focus; intrinsic-interest work helps to ensure that these are not seen as threats; employment work brings these two tendencies together. By seeing that these three types of work are quite different, have quite different motivations, and lead to quite different organizational results a climate can be generated in the company that will allow all three to find expression.

Structure

Three further types of work can be identified, which concern the structural aspect of work. These three are "product," "integration," and "control" work.

Product work is the work for which the role was set up. Generally speaking, when people think about work, they think about employment work of the product kind. If you ask a man what he does, he will answer by saying that he is a comptroller, budget analyst, market-research worker, display artist, and so on. This is employment product work. A role is set up to produce a product and product work produces it.

Integration work, on the other hand, is concerned with the limits within which the product is produced. An employee must ensure that the structure within which his product work is carried on is maintained. Unless this is done he will waste a lot of energy. Examples of integration work are: budget preparation, reviewing the salaries of subordinates, complying with government regulations, conforming to the requirements of government policies, and so on. This means that integration work will include ensuring that subordinate levels are trained in the requirements necessary to carry out their functions.

There is no doubt that work is done and energy and time used in integration work. This energy and time is diverted from producing the product of the role. As managers are frequently judged in terms of the product work they do, and not in terms of integration work, they consider integration work a waste of time and frequently neglect it.

Control work is the work that is done in order that the

results obtained can be aligned with what is required by the higher system. It includes matching resources committed to results obtained. Without adequate control work it is not possible for the president to fulfill his function of balancing the forces at work within a company. Undoubtedly the greatest need in industry is for a more adequate understanding of control work. "Management by objectives" is one way in which this is being sought after, but even so there is such a strong bias toward the belief that the best, simplest, or even the only objective for a company to have is to make a profit, that financial objectives and financial control so far outstrip the availability of other types of control that these very control devices themselves cause major distortions within a company. It is as though one attempted to control a horse by blinding it and heaving on only one rein.

Product, integration, and control work are quite different. We have said that between them they correspond with the structural mode of a company. Within a role as a holon they manifest themselves in the following ways: Product work represents the assertive mode of the role, integration work maintains the integrity of the role, and control work is required to maintain the integrity of the higher system of which the role is a part.

Within the organization these three types of work operate along three different dimensions. Product work occurs along the horizontal dimension, integration work occurs across the lateral dimension, while control work occurs in the vertical dimension. Many managers believe that work flows from the president, through higher levels of management, through lower levels and so to the shop floor. This is only true of control work.

Because many managers do not recognize this, they experience difficulties in delegating work. Not recognizing that product work flows horizontally, managers are unable to give freedom to their subordinates to act and therefore come to judge subordinates according to the way they *be-have* rather than according to the *results* they obtain. Many companies, when reviewing an organization, concentrate upon the hierarchic structure. Indeed, many believe that drawing an organization structure on a page with as few lines as possible constitutes the art of organization. Furthermore, job descriptions are behavior-oriented and not result-oriented.

Another serious problem is the fact that it is not recognized that product work at different levels is qualitatively different, and "management" is given one global definition of "getting results through others" or "plan, organize, and control," which says *how* work is done rather than *what* work is done. In other words, the emphasis is again on behavior rather than on results.

Furthermore, by recognizing that product and integration work occur in different dimensions, it can be seen that the product of one role can be the limit of another. In this way one man can truly "assist" another man to do his work by clarifying the limits within which that work is done.

The fact that the structure of a company has three dimensions implies that a three-dimensional matrix is necessary in setting up a company organization. Furthermore, it would also imply that performance should be judged on how well work is done along all three dimensions and not along one dimension only.

Process

We should now consider the final three types of work, which correspond to the process dimensions of a company. These are: transformation, project, and flux work.

Transformation work is that work which is ongoing, predictable, cyclic. Employment work of the product-transformation kind is that work which is the dominant "import/conversion/export process" which, as A. K. Rice says, is that process by which the primary tasks are performed. This is the case both for a company as well as for a role. It must be recognized, therefore, that this employment-product-transformation work is best represented by a multidimensional matrix and cannot in any way be represented by a single line. The vectoral univalent view is an oversimplification that turns the concrete complexity of the system into a meaningless abstraction.

There are many interacting transformation cycles. For example, in a gas utility there are transformation cycles of the following kind: gas systems plans are drawn up, pipelines constructed, inspections made for leaks, and maintenance work performed on the pipe. After a number of years it is removed from the ground, new systems are drawn up, and so on. Other parallel cycles occur by which gas is purchased, received from other companies, fed into the system, regulated, and passed through meters. Meters are read, customers billed, and cash received, banked, and accounted. All of this is done while employees are being recruited, screened, trained, promoted, paid, reviewed, and so on.

Some of these cycles are short while others are long, but all of the cycles are similar in being predictable, and they are all interconnected. Furthermore, transformation work is generative, that is, feedback from transformation work is part of the input for future transformation work. Because of transformation work a company endures. Transformation work is negentropic and builds up potential.

Around the transformation cycles is flux. Flux can be compared to "noise" or static in a communication system. Flux is both unpredictable, non-cyclic, and entropic—it uses up potential in the system. Examples of flux abound: the missing file, the sick employee, the accident, the unforeseen result, the failure of another part of the system to operate. The maxim "what can go wrong will go wrong" is the maxim underlying flux generation. Flux work aims at suppressing the flux, of neutralizing its ill effects.

Frequently managers think of flux work as being their main concern. As long as they are putting out fires, attending meetings, and getting ready for the next problem they feel that they are working. Flux can reach a point at which the system begins to break down. However, it must not be inferred that flux is only bad. The transformation cycles draw their raw material for growth from flux.

The environment is one of the principal sources for flux. The customer may be asked, "Please do not fold, staple, or otherwise mutilate this card," but the card nevertheless comes in folded, stapled, or otherwise mutilated. The customer is not perverse, he is simply not part of that system. He simply does not care whether the system succeeds or fails. So whereas the computer should handle about five thousand cards per minute, the whole operation comes to a halt when this particular card is fed into the machine.

Unions also are a source of flux and so are shareholders. Some union officials see the product of their roles as the generation of sufficient flux to stop the system. Furthermore, many individual employees feel that they have won if in some way they have beat the system. Shareholders can also generate flux. A phone call or letter is received: "I am a shareholder of your company . . ." and this says implicitly, "I do not care whether your systems must stop, bend or break, but I must get what I want."

However, all flux is not generated from outside and the organization itself can be set up as a flux generator. Two parts of an organization can be at odds with each other and in this way they generate flux, as does the manager who does not use a system properly, who does not follow the normal communication lines, or who mislays reports. The greatest internal flux generator within a company must surely be the staff/line organization.

In order to combat flux on a more constructive basis than simply suppressing it through flux work, many companies have taken to setting up projects. *Project work* scoops up flux and turns it into transformation work, thus raising the level of that transformation work. Projects are set up to achieve a specific objective, and when that has been achieved the project is disbanded and project work comes to a halt. Project work is a single-cycle task and has therefore a limited life span. Project work is parasitical upon the transformation cycles and there are only so many projects that can be undertaken at one time. This is quite obvious when one considers that employees most frequently made available for project work would otherwise be doing transformation work. However, it is equally important to realize that other aspects of the company are used by projects and thus speed up the deterioration of those parts.

The importance of distinguishing between transformation, product, and flux work is obvious when one undertakes to write a role description. In writing a role description it is important to concentrate upon the transformation cycle and ensure that it is clearly and adequately described. By doing this the hard skeleton of the company is established, with the employment-product-transformation cycle forming the backbone. It is only in the transformation cycles that the true pattern of an organization can be discerned, and by concentrating upon them it is possible to set down a complete picture of the company.

When writing a role description, managers who fail to distinguish between different types of work write down what comes to mind with no way of knowing whether what is written is complete. Furthermore, by not recognizing the basic underlying pattern, the manager fails to simplify the job description and avoid duplication. He establishes what is uppermost in his mind. Therefore, another person reading the description finds the whole thing incomprehensible and gets a completely different picture of the role, and this alone can be the beginning of many problems. It is not surprising, therefore, that most job descriptions are put away and forgotten after they have been written. Few are sufficiently pragmatic that they can be used as instruments in work allocation, work review, salary administration, training, and so on.

We can sum up what we have said so far with the following diagram:

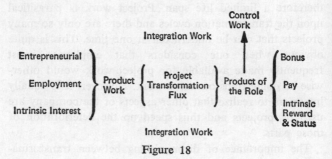

Figure 18

12. FOUR CRITERIA

I have said that the one dimensional or univalent approach is inadequate for providing a framework within which to comprehend the modern industrial complex. But how is this contention to be substantiated? By what criteria are we to judge whether or not the alternative "multivalent," or multidimensional, approach is indeed an advance?

It is evident that criteria which have their origin in dualism cannot be used to judge that which aims at going beyond dualism. Therefore the simple tests of measurement, statistical interpretation, and manipulation—the mathematical process generally—cannot be used. Any attempt to reduce organization simply to a set of axioms, deductions, and conclusions leads us far from the field of battle where the issues are being decided. The very basis of work is, as we shall see, *the dilemma*. Dualism assumes that a situation is self-consistent, but this is not the case. Life is not self-consistent at all.

The way a man organizes his experience and the way he organizes work are the same. Experience and organization are isomorphic. A theory is experience made articulate. Therefore, the problem of finding adequate criteria for determining the acceptability of the approach is not academic but of vital importance because if we are successful, we shall, at the same time, *discover criteria by which to judge the acceptability of an organization*. The popular notion is that if a company makes a profit, i.e., a return on the shareholder's investment, the organization is acceptable. But this is the very point at issue; the very notion of profit itself is being challenged, as well as its acceptability as a criterion.

A company's success is judged at present along a single dimension: the criterion of profit. Professor Dale[1] says that a manager may not even have the right to consider any other criteria, unless he believes that to do so will contribute to profit making. In other words, profit is used not only as a practical criterion but as a moral imperative.

It is often claimed that the profit criterion is the best because it is simple, and on the face of it, it is indeed simple: At the end of the year one has but to balance income against expenditure and ask oneself whether the remainder could have been made equally well by investing one's capital elsewhere. This sort of accounting is good at best for the corner-store grocer and has but minimal value for a large company.

The confusion surrounding the word "profit" is brought out well in the book *Profits in Modern Economy* in which the writers state: "What constitutes profit, how profit should be measured and how profits contribute to a healthy and vigorous economy, lead to frequent disagreement and confusion. . . . When a representative of business, labor, or government is discussing profit, he is likely to select the usage which supports his point of view."[2] It would seem, then, that the profit criterion is not simple at all. It is probable that when people say that it is simple they mean that profit as a criterion is unquestioned and least likely to raise controversy. In other words, the criterion of profit has the simplicity of a dogma.

Even were the concept of profit not vague and complex, even were it clear and distinct, this in itself would not be sufficient justification for its use. All too frequently the simplicity of a criterion, objective, or solution is confused with its value.

There is a story of a man who lost his key and was searching for it under a lighted lamppost when his neighbor passed by. His neighbor offered to help look and asked the man where he had dropped the key. The man nodded toward some bushes hidden in shadow. "Then why not look over there?" asked his neighbor, somewhat surprised.

"Don't you see, there is more light here," the man re-torted.

The legitimacy of the profit criterion had its origins with the entrepreneur. For the entrepreneur who owns and operates the business, profit may be the only criterion he feels justified in consulting; it may be legitimate for him to consider the company as a one dimensional situation. But the professional manager must be able to widen his perspective and recognize that other dimensions must find expression if he is to operate successfully and in such a way that he will find his own life meaningful.

Many managers believe that a theoretical framework for an understanding of organization is, at best, a luxury; at worst, a waste of time. They say that organization is sim-ply a "seat of the pants" affair and that the less involved one becomes in theory, the better. By this they imply that there is no common structure underlying organization.

Most company organizations stem from the opinions of the chief executive, or someone appointed by him, on the way that people should work together. Such opinions are of value only if: (1) they correspond to a wider set of criteria and by this are elevated from opinion to science; or (2) they can be enforced. By virtue of the economic power that he wields, the chief executive can coerce others to share his opinion. However, if his opinion does not cor-respond to a wider set of criteria, this enforcement will, sooner or later, bring in its wake increased problems, addi-tional work, or illness, either to himself, or more likely, to those working for him. A criterion, or set of criteria, of ex-cellence is therefore of paramount importance if organi-zation is to acquire objectivity.

I suggest that there are four criteria by which to judge an organization which are the same four criteria that were traditionally used to judge the value of a scientific theory. More recently these criteria have fallen into disuse because of the increasing emphasis that has been given to process and the consequent decline in interest in structure. For ex-ample, science currently favors "operational" definitions and boundary definitions. With the renewed interest in structure and an increasing recognition of the "ecology of science," it is likely the four criteria will regain popularity. In view of our contention that the way we structure our experience and the way we structure an organization have a common origin, it will not come as a surprise that the same criteria are common to both. These criteria are: *simplicity, completeness, pragmatism, and communicability.*

Simplicity

The criterion of simplicity requires that the minimum number of assumptions be postulated. This criterion is also known as Occam's razor: *Entities are not to be multiplied without necessity.* This implies that each assumption or element in the theory is independent. This is the law of parsimony, which has played such an important part in eradicating unnecessary ideas and has enabled science to advance.

The best organization is the simplest, that is, the one with the minimum number of roles, and therefore the minimum overlap existing between them. This criterion of simplicity is also important in considering the number of levels that an organization should have, as well as the reporting relationship that should exist between them.

It is important to distinguish simplicity from ease as these two are frequently confused in people's minds. Ease means that which requires the least effort and is associated with the most familiar, the habitual. The word simple derives from the notion of one or unity. The simple, the aesthetic, and the economic are all different aspects of the same quality.

Completeness

It is not enough that a theory or an organization's structure be simple. The criterion of completeness requires that all the facts that are available are included within the scientific theory. The inadequacy of a theory is frequently brought to light by uncovering facts that lie outside the range of the theory that purports to explain them. For many years Newton's physics formed the framework for physicists, but to an increasing degree facts and observations arose which were not easily incorporated in the theory. The structure suffered increasingly until Einstein developed a higher level theory capable of incorporating not only what Newton's theory had already encompassed, but the new troublesome facts as well.

In an organization the bulk of the major tasks that have to be accomplished are easily and readily incorporated within almost any kind of organization structure. It is those few remaining tasks that test or prove the adequacy of the organization, just in the same way as it is the exception that tests or proves the rule.

Not only should the organization be capable of incorporating tasks that need to be performed at the time it is set up, it should also be capable of adjusting to and assimilating new tasks that arise.

The criteria of simplicity and completeness concern the excellence of the system itself. They are concerned with the inner workings of the theory. Science develops through thesis (the simple), antithesis (the complete), to synthesis (a higher level thesis). It is now necessary to consider two other criteria: pragmatism/heuristic and communicability. Both of these test the extent to which the system —the theory of organization—is self-transcendent. That is, they are concerned with the external workings of the theory.

Pragmatism

The pragmatic or heuristic criterion is that which tests the theory's ability to go beyond itself and say something about the environment. Its simplest formula is "does it work?" Scientific method, through experiments, conducts a search for relations and structure in the empirical world. The scientific structure, through theories, principles, and laws "produces languages of some structure." "If the two structures are similar, the theories work."[3] In its purest form, the pragmatic principle says that concepts and statements that are not empirically verifiable should have no place in a physical theory. Some believe this to be the only test of scientific validity. But if it were so, it would lead to a sterility and deadness in scientific reasoning, and it would mean that the sudden leap to new insights would be more rare because it would be more hazardous.

The pragmatic criterion is much beloved of the businessman. It is invariably the only one invoked in a conscious way. His test is "does it work?" There appears to be something real, virile, and down-to-earth about such a question, although it is not always clear what the question means.

Profitability is the pragmatic criterion par excellence. Profitability *could be* an acceptable criterion to the shareholder. However, the inconsistency of the profit criterion in such a limited sense with a manager's basic motivation has been clearly pointed out by Galbraith who says that the large modern corporation is controlled by its management. The managerial revolution is accepted. As long as earnings are above a certain minimum, management has little to fear from its stockholder. Yet it is for these stockholders—remote, powerless, and unknown—that management seeks to maximize its profit. *Profit maximization involves a substantial contradiction. Those in charge forgo personal reward to enhance it for others.*[4] It is therefore useful to recognize what a manager means when he says that a company must be profitable. He is most likely invoking the pragmatic criterion. It seems that he is saying that a company must do well what it intends to do. But because he has been conditioned into the use of a single dimensional approach, he only knows how to say this by using the language of profit.

Probably the most "workable" theory is the one that enables the environment to be modified in a predictable way. Managers intuitively feel this and, working only with the pragmatic criterion, will judge an organization in relation to its ability to "achieve goals." The notion of goal achievement is paradoxically based upon a static theory. It is based upon the closed systems theory of organization. In this theory it is believed that one has to set goals because (it is felt) it is necessary to disturb the equilibrium within an organization in order to be able to get any work done at all. There must be many managers who are familiar with the frustrating exercise of "setting goals." Hours can be spent upon this with considerable frustration and conflict among those participating. In the end, after the goals have been set, they are put to one side and the managers return to their normal work. Often the goals are never mentioned again.

The pragmatic criterion is undoubtedly important. Because its importance is so well known it is not necessary to justify it. However, to regard it as the only criterion can lead to considerable confusion.

Communicability

The last criterion, that of communicability, is the test of the system's ability to "mesh" with or fit into a higher system. If a new theory in a given branch of science is propounded, that theory must mesh with the other theories in that science in order for it to be acceptable. Quotations and footnotes to a paper or a book are important for showing how the theory meshes in with the higher system.

It could be said that the scientist's need to reduce data to quantitative terms is an aspect of this need to have a new theory mesh with existing theories. Undoubtedly many phenomena and explanation about them are kept outside the scientific pale because they do not lend themselves to quantitative statements.

Likewise, "meshing" is important in an organization. In setting up a new department or role, the question of whether or not it fits in with the existing structure is undoubtedly a test of how well the role is organized. However, it is an interesting reflection on us that we shift the onus for fitting-in to the role incumbent. If we are to have a greater regard for structure, we should likewise have a regard for this criterion, particularly bearing in mind that a system requires the mutual relatedness of its parts.

13. CENTER AND PERIPHERY— THE BASIC POLARITY

Our study so far has been concerned with what we might call the *"statics"* of organization, its structure, and process framework. The paradigms that have been developed have shown how parts of the organization interact and make up a multifaceted but unified whole. We have shown that the structure underlying this interaction is basically simple. But so far our work is only half complete. We have not yet come to grips with "commitment," "capacity" and "discretion." We have explored the limits of work, but not the discretion exercised within those limits. We shall therefore be concerned now with the *dynamics* of a company. Framework is the self-limitation of will, and we must understand this as the dynamic of life and the dynamic of work.

It is fairly obvious that an organization cannot exist without people, and yet the implications of this fact can be easily overlooked. Organizations must be designed with people in mind, yet all too often organization theorists, as well as management practitioners, direct their attention solely to the "goals" or "objectives" of the organization, to specific functions that must be performed, to principles of organization, or, worse still, to different ways of drawing organization charts. The notion that work is a natural outcome of the way that people are made and that the problem is understanding how to channel this work in such a way that it is not wasted is not generally realized. To understand the dynamics of organization we must understand human nature, at least to the extent that we are thereby able to relate human nature to an organization. This does not mean that a manager must be a psychologist. He is not required to manipulate or tamper with the psychic make-up of people who work for him, but he must know a sufficient amount about human nature to know what can and what cannot be done.

Elliott Jaques has been responsible for showing how the psychological make-up of people profoundly affects organization behavior. A medical doctor, doctor of philosophy, and psychoanalyst, Jaques has been the socio-analyst of a company, the Glacier Metal Industry, for about twenty years, and a whole school of management is evolving from his findings. Jaques has had many original insights into the problem of management and much of his work will require years of development. He believes that psychoanalysis can provide the framework for describing human nature in a way that can be understood by managers and so enable them to take it into account in a conscious, rational way when considering problems of organization.[1]

Dr. Harry Levinson has shown in his writings, and particularly in his book *The Exceptional Executive*,[2] how so many of the Freudian insights into the psychological mechanisms are of great value in helping toward an understanding of organization behavior.

The point of view that is adopted in this book is that of Zen Buddhism which, with its down-to-earth approach, its insistence upon the concrete situation, and its grasp of the real essentials of life and action, is particularly suitable to the Western business mind. It is possible to reach the insights afforded by Zen without undergoing any specialized study of the theory that some writers have built on and around it. Zen does not invalidate the findings of psychoanalysis, but it does enable it to become divested of its parochial, clinical trappings and move from a limited, medical school of thought to a more universal understanding. Furthermore, Zen enables psychoanalysis in its practical aspects to move from an exotic, quasi-therapeutic, and extremely expensive practice to an accessible, growth-oriented one. Erich Fromm, a psychoanalyst who was an exponent of the Zen viewpoint, said that Zen "can have a most fertile and clarifying influence on the theory and technique of psychoanalysis."[3]

It has been said that conflict and tension are not necessarily undesirable within an organization. Indeed, the dimensions of the company are such that, to the extent that they are delegated as clearly as possible, they will generate conflict. This conflict will provide the basis for growth in the company, provided that it is given the opportunity to be expressed in a meaningful way. Discretion is capacity in action, and we can now define capacity as the *power to perceive ideas that will resolve conflict in such a way as to enable growth, expansion, and self-regulation to occur.*

Freudian psychoanalytical theory is based upon the notion of conflict, and the techniques of psychoanalysis are designed to bring the patient into a positive rather than a negative relationship with this conflict. Zen likewise is concerned with bringing about this positive relationship with conflict. However, psychoanalysis sees conflict as something that is acquired through life experience. Zen sees the conflict as one manifestation of a universal polarity. The Freudian would see conflict as an undesirable accident and therefore something to be "treated," while Zen would see conflict as the basis of all opportunity. According to Zen, conflict is not something that arises in childhood and is progressively dealt with thereafter. On the contrary, the conflict does not have its origin in time, but has its origin in the basic polarity. It is in time that the effects of the conflict are worked out because *the working out of conflict creates time.*

To understand work, organization, growth, human motivation, the urge toward power, the difference between capacity and ability—to understand those very questions that press so heavily upon us as managers for solution—we must understand conflict: first as it exists within an individual, and then as it is found in organizations. In both cases, we must see conflict as a highly disruptive influence *and* as the only true source of growth. As an aid in understanding this difficult problem, we shall first make a very brief reference to Freud's understanding of the basic conflict, or basic polarity within man. It will be necessary to subject Freud's approach to some critical analysis in order to bring out the significance of the deeper insight that Zen provides, but this critical analysis is not intended in any way to be exhaustive, nor is it intended to denigrate the work of a very great mind.

The word "individual" means undivided. It is a word that is often used when referring to a single person. Most people look upon themselves as one, as a unity. This oneness or unity is, however, for most of us but a potential. Instead of being one, we are two; in the very core of our being we are divided against ourselves. From being two comes a profound sense of separateness and a longing to be complete. This longing in its turn gives rise to restlessness, to the urge to do, and from this come the various activities of men. Indeed, this would appear to be the origin of the activities of all life, and perhaps even of the universe itself, because this "two-ness" is not confined to man only, but is a fundamental pattern pervading all things.

Freud recognized that "two-ness" is fundamental in man and ascribed man's difficulties to it. But he was very ambivalent about its origin and gave several reasons for its presence in man. We said earlier that the company is a whole and that this wholeness is an expression of will, of the urge to grow to self-realization inherent in man. In Freudian theory this unity is the outcome of blind "unknown and uncontrollable forces"[4] which Freud called the Id. In opposition to the Id is the Ego, which holds the Id in check. It is that part of the Id which is modified by the direct influence of the external world. Freud likened the relationship between these two to the relationship between a rider and a horse, with the difference that whereas the rider would use his own strength, the ego would use borrowed forces. Thus, an opposition exists between the two in which the ego "endeavours to substitute the reality principle for the pleasure principle which reigns supreme in the Id."[5]

However, Freud did not look upon the Ego-Id opposition as being fundamental, but gave at different times two other origins of the fundamental conflict. The two origins are the Oedipus complex and the polarity of instincts. The Oedipus complex arises when the son develops an attachment to his mother and at the same time is identified with his father. This gives rise to the triad, boy-father-mother. The attachment and identification can exist side by side until "the sexual wishes in regard to the mother become more intense and the father is perceived as an obstacle to them."[6]

Freud believed that the Oedipus complex was the prototype of all psychological conflicts and, therefore, that the attachment/identification polarity was the basic polarity within the individual. This is so much the case that Freud felt that religion and morality, that which the overwhelming majority of mankind have always considered to arise out of what is highest in man, "were acquired phylogenetically out of the father complex."[7] "Religion and moral restraint come from the actual process of mastering the Oedipus complex itself and social feelings from the necessity for overcoming the rivalry that then remained between members of the younger generation."[8] Thus, out of an original unity—Id or It—a polarity arises. But this polarity is acquired, it has its origin in time, and because of this man is made a prisoner of the world. He is locked into the world and can hope for nothing beyond the world.

Freud modified his position later when he said that the primary conflict arises from the basic instinctual forces being divided into two opposing instincts: Eros and Thanatos. Life, according to Freud, is *a conflict and compromise* [author's italics]. The problem of the origin of life would remain a cosmological one; and the problem of the purpose and goal of life would be answered dualistically." Freud said later that "both instincts would be active in every particle of living substance, although in unequal proportions."[9] This statement makes the Oedipus theory redundant.

Our contention is that the basic polarity of man is not acquired, but is that which makes man possible; it does not arise from experience, but makes experience necessary. Experience has as its framework time and space, and yet these in turn are projections of the intensive-extensive modes of the holon of man; they arise out of the self-limitation of will. The Will, or Id, is divided against itself, and this gives rise to the basic conflict. This conflict is reconciled by a primordial Idea, and out of this idea time, space, and, therefore, existence become possible.

The Will, or Id, which is the "source of those unknown and uncontrollable forces by which we are lived," has two modes of being that are mutually dependent but mutually antagonistic. The Will and the two inferior principles, a supernal triad, are *not existing,* but form the source of existence.

However, in so far as the two inferior principles have a structure that can be revealed, they can be considered *to be.* This structure is the structure of "being-the-center" and "being-the-periphery."[10] Will manifests as center *and* as periphery simultaneously because Will is individual and cannot be divided. But the two modes of being are mutually exclusive, and consequently a conflict is inherent within Will. This conflict is not something accidental or acquired and cannot be eliminated. As long as Will manifests, it manifests as center and periphery. Experience arises out of these two modes of being; they themselves cannot be experienced. Experience is therefore polarized and has for its basic poles *perception* and *action.*

To adopt a descriptive approach, it could be said that "I" see myself as center of the world and in doing so see the world as periphery. But in so far as I see *the world,* the world is center and I am periphery. These two mutually exclusive modes of being arise and, because the Will is one and undivided, strive to reblend into a whole. This very striving itself represents another mode of being: the mode of being of existence. (It is interesting to note that existence comes from the Latin *"ex sistere"* meaning "to stand outside of").

To say that "I" see myself as "center" is a rough approximation of what occurs because at this level "I" is not. "I" is the striving which through "conflict and compromise" conciliates the primary polarity. "I" is a striving. By being center, "I am" is asserted; by being periphery "Am I?" is questioned. *"I am I?" is the primary word.* "I am" is the expression of the individuality of Will.

As center, Will *perceives;* as periphery, Will *acts.* The idea "center-periphery" is the primary perception. The expression of this idea "I am I?" is the primary action. The "subject-verb-predicate" relationship discloses the primary structure of being, a structure in which there is an inherent polarity.

The primary duality is not *in* consciousness. In much the same way that electric light is the outcome of an energy passing across positive and negative elements, so consciousness is the outcome of the energy of will traversing the center-periphery polarity. Indeed, consciousness is regarded as subjective light, and light as objective consciousness. Consciousness is also a striving in that it is consciousness of something, and that of which one is conscious is both in doubt and yet a promise of what will resolve the doubt. Doubt is the unknown, the darkness—it is ultimately Hell; promise is light, it is ultimately Heaven. The world is the interplay of light and darkness, known and unknown.

In order to make the difficult point of center and periphery a little more clear, the following is offered. It should, however, be remembered that it is simply an illustration designed to point to the principles that lie beyond.

If I observe myself impartially, I will notice that all perceptions come to me from the four quarters of the universe. If I am at sea or in the prairies, I have a vivid impression of being at the center of the earth which is spread out around me like a huge plate. This centrality can be shown in yet another way. At the moment there are probably hundreds of thousands of people dying of starvation and yet I give this fact little thought. If I were told that thousands of people in New York or Toronto were dying,

I would probably become more concerned. I would become even more concerned were I told that hundreds were dying in the town in which I lived, and yet more concerned still if I were told that the entire street of people around me had been wiped out. Greater concern yet would arise were I told that a member of my family was dying. The closer the calamity gets, the more important it becomes to me.

This change in importance as a consequence of perspective can also be seen in time. We are little concerned about the catastrophes of one hundred thousand years ago, or even a hundred years ago, but as events approach in time—ten years, ten months, or ten days—these events acquire an increasing importance.

I am here and now, and here and now the universe begins and ends. Wherever I am, the world is alive; as I walk around the world lights up; and as I pass by the world grows dim.

Yet this is not the full story. I am at the mercy of the world. Should I be in a restaurant and find that I do not have money to pay for the food I have eaten, or should I go to the doctor and he says, "Remove your clothes," I see that I am no longer the center. I feel that I am nothing, or at the best an object. *I see that I am at the periphery of the world, the center of which lies outside me somewhere.* The boss says, "Come and see me," and I go. Each of us knows that we are to die and yet feels certain that the universe will not die with us. The fact that the center lies outside of me in an unattainable distance is shown very clearly by perspective lines receding and meeting at a distant center. These perspective lines are used by artists, particularly the surrealists, to give a poignant sense of our being lost, separated from our source—out of touch with our center and in a dreamworld.

It is true that we *are* at the center of the universe, and this is given as a matter of immediate observation; it is also true that we *are* at the periphery of the universe, and this, also, is a matter of immediate observation. The sense of living in infinite space and time comes from the center having no periphery; the sense of alienation comes from the periphery having no center. This primary polarity is the basis of our joy and suffering. To the extent that we see ourselves as unconditioned at the center or fully conditioned at the periphery, we approximate inward release. To the extent that we see ourselves as both at the center and at the periphery simultaneously, we suffer. The drama of life is an outcome of the attempts that we make to resolve the conflict by either suppressing one or other of these poles, or by so valuing the one pole over the other that the conflict is laid to rest.

"The search to be at the center is the nostalgia for paradise. By this we mean to find oneself always and without effort in the center of the world, at the heart of reality; and by a short cut and in a natural manner to transcend the human condition and to recover the divine condition—as the Christians would say, the condition before the fall."[11]

There is a search to be at the periphery which is no less ardent than the search to be at the center. A search that is no less "religious." In science the role of the observer, the center, has been eliminated, or at best "conventionalized and stylized," and the periphery is all.

The alternative is not a relativism in which the two extremes are merged in a dull porridge gray. Compromise is bad faith. The burden of this primary duality is the cross of man on which he is permanently crucified and from which he is eternally resurrected through a striving which is life. Zen expresses man's dilemma thus:

> It is like a man up a tree hanging from a branch with his mouth. His hands can't grasp the bough, his feet won't reach one. Under the tree there is another man who asks him the meaning of life. If he doesn't answer, he evades his duty. If he answers, he will lose his life. What should he do?

Buddha taught, "All is suffering,"[12] and the suffering arises out of the unending conflict through the constant experience of being the center and the periphery simultaneously. The existential anxiety that underlies our lives derives from this primary duality.

Existential anxiety is characterized by having no form. It is anxiety about anxiety. It arises through the center perceiving itself as its own periphery and the periphery vanishing constantly within its own center. The sense of the mind annihilating the mind can lead to the most unbearable horror. It is a state that few can stand, and it is only the brave who will try to pass beyond this numb desert to the reconciliation of the opposites that lies beyond. Most people turn their backs and find a form for their anxiety. This form has three variations: the fear of death (which is the fear of the loss of the center); the fear of madness (which is the fear of being alone); and the meeting of these two fears in the fear of failure. The fear of failure is expressed in insecurity, which arises when the striving falters and the integrity begins to disintegrate.

Our fears are all of our own making. We know this but must avoid the responsibility for it. To assume the responsibility lays us open to the threat that one tug of the thread can unravel our whole scheme of life. This avoidance of responsibility is what the psychologist calls "projection."

I therefore project a world that is a reflection of the primary word[13] "I am I?" It has two basic characteristics: a possibility that I must search for and a certainty that I must avoid. The possibility that I must seek is a projection of the periphery; it is the projection of "I am." In the search for this possibility I seek an identity, and I seek this in power, possessions, prestige, or a sense of belonging.[14] The certainty I must avoid is the projection of the not-self, the enemy. Wherever I am I have the enemy, and this enemy is always *someone*. This projection is the mechanism by which the ego is created, which is always founded on ambition. Ego is an ambition, and this ambition is to realize my basic possibility and finally to overcome my enemy.

It is the possibility of this projection of the world that

makes man different from animals. This possibility first
finds expression in language, for in language the duality is
first given form. An animal, no less than man, has the
duality center and periphery. The animal, however, is unable to express this duality in language. Language does not
exist because of the need to communicate. The need and
ability to communicate can exist quite separately from
language.[15] The "word" arises through the possibility inherent in the human being to project—and therefore to hypos-
tatize and thereby neutralize—the primary duality.[16] But
the "word," the fact, only becomes such when it is
received. Language is a superimposition on communication
of the inherent possibility to project the primary duality as
the primary word. Oswald Spengler, in *Decline of the
West,*[17] states that the mere naming of time was an unparalleled deliverance. How much more of a deliverance
must it have been to have been able to name the primary
duality?

But language also bears the burden of this duality, this

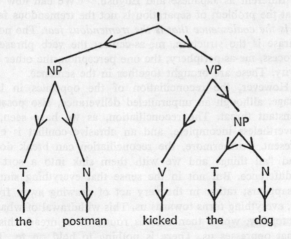

(modified after Chomsky). I: idea. NP: noun phrase
VP: verb phrase. T: article. N: noun. V: verb.

Figure 19

ambiguity. Spengler says that root words seem to have appeared in pairs. The analysis that Noam Chomsky does of language bears out this dualistic nature of language.

The above diagram appears in *The Ghost in the Machine* by Koestler and he says that "this is about the simplest schema for generating a sentence. At the apex of the inverted tree is I—it might be an idea, a visual image, the intention of saying something—which is not yet verbally articulated. Let us call this the I stage. Then the two main branches of the tree shoot out, the doer and his doing, which at the I stage was still experienced as an individual unit, are split into different speech categories, noun phrase and verb phrase. This separation must be a tremendous feat of abstraction for the child—how can you separate the cat from the grin, or the kick from the postman?—yet it is a universal property of all known languages; and it is with precisely this feat of 'abstract thinking' that the child starts its adventure in language at a very early age, in languages as different as Japanese and English."[18] We can now see that the problem of separation is not the tremendous feat. *It is the coalescence that is the tremendous feat.* The noun phrase is the structure, me-as-center; the verb phrase is process, me-as-periphery; the one perception, the other activity. These are brought together in the sentence.

However, the reconciliation of the opposites in language, although an unparalleled deliverance, also poses a constant threat. The reconciliation, as we have seen, is nevertheless incomplete, and an abrasive conflict is ever present. Furthermore, the reconciliation can break down and "all things and we with them sink into a sort of indifference. But not in the sense that everything simply disappears; rather in the very act of drawing away from us, everything turns towards us. This withdrawal of what is in totality, which then crowds round us in dread, this is what oppresses us. There is nothing to hold on to. The only thing that remains and overwhelms us whilst what is slips away is this 'Nothing.' "[19]

Underlying the deliverance, therefore, is the threat, and

the threat can be overcome only by labor. Man was innocent in the Garden of Eden until eating the fruit of the tree that was "to be desired to make one wise." (Genesis 3:6.) The creation of language was the original sin; its promise was paradise, the price, eternal labor. Since he first created language, man has struggled to overcome the tyranny of his own creation.

The primary polarity is therefore basic to language and as such basic to the most widespread and most fundamental of human creations. This polarity is, therefore, not an accident that has occurred to man, but an essential ingredient of man.

14. TERRITORY AND THE MANAGER

Our study leads to the conclusion that there is a basic polarity underlying all of man's activities, indeed all activities of life—being simultaneously at the center and at the periphery of the world. Our problem is to show how an understanding of this polarity affects organization and work. How are we to interpret the fact that one's life consists of coping with this polarity through creation, compromise, and conflict?

To answer this question, we shall first refer to some studies in animal behavior, particularly those by Robert Ardrey.[1] The value of studying animals is that they display simplified versions of behavior which are sometimes found to be common to human beings. The conclusion to be drawn from these studies is not that man is "nothing but" an animal, but rather that man has woven these common units of behavior into the tapestry of his life. If life is a system, then the elements of this system are units of behavior which, in their interrelationship, give rise to variations and mutations according to the level of the integrating force or idea.

Animals as well as man have the problem of reconciling the opposites of center and periphery. Although this statement cannot be "proven," it can be inferred from the behavior of animals, and perhaps the best basis for such inference can be found in the "look." Jean Paul Sartre bases almost the whole of his philosophy on the polarity inherent in the existential situation. Sartre deals extensively with the Other, and in particular with the Other manifested in the "look." The Other looking at me increases the tension inherent in the center/periphery polarity. This look indeed exemplifies the polarity. As Sartre points out, "the Other is not only the one whom I see, but the one *who sees me.*"[2] "I recognize that *I am* as the Other sees me."[3] The Other is manifestly a center who has me for his periphery; and yet the Other is a periphery to my center. "The appearance of the Other in the world corresponds therefore to a fixed sliding of the whole universe, to a decentralization of the world which undermines the centralization which I am simultaneously affecting."[4]

Konrad Lorenz, a very perceptive ethologist, also deals briefly with the problem of the "look" in his book *Man Meets Dog.* He says, "Animals only look at each other fixedly when they intend to take drastic measures or are afraid of each other. Consequently they conceive a prolonged, fixed gaze as being something hostile and threatening and rate it in man as the expression of extreme malevolence."[5]

Although animals also have the problem of center and periphery, they do not have language, that is, a structure by which this polarity may be hypostatized. Thus, an animal has three principal structures by which it resolves the center/periphery polarity: by territory, status, and pairing. We shall first deal with territory and show how it is an outcome of the center/periphery polarity, and then attempt to show how it relates to the behavior of men in organizations. Then we shall deal with status and its organizational counterpart of hierarchy. The pair is not a device widely used in industry in the Western world, but Shigeru Kobayashi refers to it as a mode of behavior in Japanese industry, and, in that it can neutralize some of the tension inherent in the basic polarity, it is a noteworthy structure. We shall therefore make brief reference to it at the end of this chapter.

Territory

"A territory," says Ardrey, "is an area of space, whether of water or earth or air, which an animal or group of animals defend as an exclusive preserve. In most, but not all, territorial species, defense is directed against fellow members of the kind."[6]

The need to possess territory seems to be fundamental, even more fundamental than the need for sexual relations. With the need for territory comes, naturally, the need to identify the boundary or periphery, for it is because of the presence of the boundary as well as of the center that a territory can be said to exist. Setting up a territory is both an individual act as well as a social act; that is, an act of establishing the "self" and the "other."

We have grown accustomed to the belief that the sexual need is the most fundamental need of man and animals. This acceptance has been due primarily to the widespread appeal of psychoanalysis. However, the studies of the ethologists leave no doubt that for territorial animals territory, not sex, is fundamental. "Male animals compete for real estate, never for females. . . . The male who has not gained a territory on the stamping ground is sexually unmotivated . . . Within the arena some properties have greater sexual value than others. . . . The female is sexually unresponsive to any male who has not succeeded in gaining territory. The doe is attracted and excited by the qualities of the property, not the qualities of the proprietor."[7]

The value of a given territory comes from its position: the more central it is the higher its value. Among the cobs, for example, "only a super cob lasts long on a center territory." Possession of a territory does not arise out of concern for food because in many cases animals graze elsewhere than on their territory. When it is further recognized that it is as important to identify a boundary as it is to establish it, not as defiance but in order to *reduce* hostility, it becomes evident that territory has something more than mere survival value. Animals that are in possession of territory acquire enhanced energy and a challenger to the possession is almost always defeated. It is even on record that a male cob with a broken leg nevertheless successfully held on to his territory for eight days. In modern industrial jargon this would be equivalent to saying that the possessor of territory is "well motivated." But how can this be explained?

A clue to the answer of this question is given by the behavior of the herring gull and the stickleback. Both chase an intruder from their territory and will pursue it into its own territory. At this point the retreating one will turn and take the offensive, pursuing the erstwhile pursuer back into his own territory. Again the point will come when the tables are turned. This will continue until they come to glower at each other across the border. At this point both sticklebacks will suddenly "while goggling at each other in loathing, stand on their heads and dig holes in the sand." The herring gulls, too, will reach the point of facing each other across the border: "Since they face each other not two feet apart, yet both are gripped by ferocity's storm, any observation will predict instant battle. But there will be no battle. Both gulls instead will suddenly, murderously, start pulling up grass."[8]

This behavior is instructive from two standpoints. Territorial combats are not life-and-death struggles. Rarely do the combatants kill each other. On the contrary, the aim seems to be to humiliate rather than to hurt the opponent; to cause the opponent shame. "The urge to preserve prestige and dignity is not specifically human, but lies deep in the instinctive layers of the mind which, in the higher animals, are closely related to our own." Animals have a specific propitiating gesture and it is rare that one animal will attack another displaying this propitiating gesture. Thus, the combat is also mainly a psychological one in which "simple ear-lowering, horn-waggling, or other stern displays" are frequently enough to discourage the challenge.

"Off the stamping ground the gladiators display no antagonism. Should a hungry enough lion appear, the first to spot it gives a stiff legged hopping signal alerting his fellows. All retire by customary paths to wait amicably until the lion goes away."[9]

Secondly, the nearer to the center of his territory that an animal finds himself, the greater security and therefore psychological strength that he seems to derive. This is easily derived from the chase of the sticklebacks. Ardrey quotes another ethologist, Frank Darling: "I would like to put forward the hypothesis that one of the important functions of territory is the provision of periphery—periphery being defined as that kind of edge where there is another bird of the same specie occupying a territory. By pushing up against each other, rather than spreading themselves out, the birds are giving themselves peripheries. The breeding ground . . . is a place with two focal points, the nest and the periphery."[10] This is what Ardrey calls the "castle and border" interpretation of territory. "There is the castle or nest or heartland or lair to provide security, and just as important, the border region where the fun goes on. These are basic needs of a psychological order, for security and for stimulation, and under normal circumstances they would conflict. The territorial principle has however satisfied both without loss to either."[11] The territorial principle has, in our terms, provided for a center or "a nest," and a periphery, a border—the basic polarity reconciled in territory. It is this that accounts for one of the most interesting things about territorial behavior: "the possession of territory lends enhanced energy to the proprietor." The "psychological" advantage that the proprietor has over the challenger is just that advantage of having reconciled the two opposing points of view by being "somewhere." Through possessing territory, the opposition is for the moment laid to rest.

On the other hand, by the very act of challenge, the challenger is in doubt; a conflict is present. The advantage of the challenged is precisely the disadvantage of the challenger; let the challenged show but a moment of doubt and the advantage is lost, the territory is open for spoils. The "simple ear-lowering, horn-waggling, or other stern display" must have authority, it must come from a reconciled duality before it is "enough to discourage the challenge."[12]

Displacement behavior is an excellent example of how a third factor, that of building a nest, for example, can be a perfectly satisfactory way of resolving the center/periphery conflict. The existence of the Other makes for a periphery until the Other challenges, until he "looks," whereupon the Other becomes a center and so awakens the basic conflict with all its stress. Thus, two birds confronting each other are physical manifestations of the primary duality. This duality is reconciled by a third force. In the case of the gulls and sticklebacks referred to above, this third factor is the nest; in the case of human beings, *this third factor is the "word."*

Thus, territory seems to be a basic need of life, and as this is so, where must we look for satisfaction of this need in human beings? Traditionally, "a man's home was his castle." Ownership of land was a direct manifestation of the territorial need. The "trespassers will be prosecuted" notices plaguing the countryside are but the counterparts of the wolf's hind leg. However, ownership of land is no longer possible for the majority of the urban populations of the world. The majority of people in the industrial world no longer own territory of a physical kind. Yet if this need for territory is so important and so widespread, it must find some outlet. There must be some surrogate, some means for sublimating the "psychic energy" that is aroused through the territorial "instinct." In the industrial world, therefore, men are in the process of establishing a new form of territory: *that of the role.* A company is itself an arena in which males, and to an increasing degree females, *vie for territory.* A market is an arena in which companies vie for territory. Territorial behavior sheds light on behavior at work as well as the behavior manifested by companies competing with each other for markets.

A role has both a center and a periphery. The center of a role is the product idea for the expression of which the role is established. We have called this the product of the role. On the other hand, the role has a periphery, and it is at the periphery of the role that interaction is possible with other roles in a company.

The boundary is very important, both for a role and a territory, as is the ability to mark out the boundary. Nature has established a variety of ways by which territorial boundaries can be established. "At the level of cells, organ, and organism the boundary sub-systems are cell membranes, organ capsules, and the skin or outer covering. The sub-systems are protective against unwanted input, yet permeable to specific sorts of matter, energy, and information. At all levels of social systems the geographical borders, or limits of the systems territory, and its boundary sub-systems are different. The boundary sub-system is usually found along the periphery of the territory. It is made up of individual organisms, groups, or organizations which maintain the integrity, or which control the passage into or out of energy or material or messages."[13]

The boundary of a role provides stimulation and most of a company's politics are concerned with border disputations. "There are always relationships, roles, and policies in organization, but often they are not explicit. When they are not, there is endless possibility for the need for political maneuver; there are jealousies, misunderstandings, frustrations and conflict."[14]

A British organization theorist has emphasized the importance of the boundary. He says that "the effectiveness of every intergroup relationship is determined by the extent to which groups involved have to defend themselves against uncertainty about the integrity of boundaries."[15] Task management is, according to him, essentially the definition of boundaries between task systems and the control of transactions across these boundaries. Without adequate boundary definition for activity systems and sentient groups, organization boundaries are difficult to define. Frontier skirmishing is inevitable. It is, he says, perhaps a major paradox of modern complex enterprises that the more certainly boundaries can be located, the more easily formal communication systems can be established. Unless a boundary is adequately located, different people will draw it in different places and hence there will be confusion between inside and outside. In the individual this confusion leads to breakdown, and in the enterprise to inefficiency and failure. If chaos is defined as uncertainty about boundary definition, or more colloquially, as not knowing who or what belongs where, then every transaction is potentially chaotic. "If we go further and suggest that the major characteristic of disaster is the obliteration of known boundaries, of the guides and directories which govern existence, then every transaction can be said to have built into it the elements of insipient disaster. To be continuously confused about role person boundaries, or completely unable to define and maintain boundaries, is to be *mentally sick*." [16]

Reference was made earlier to three forms of conflict within a company. It was said the first form of conflict arises out of the nature of organization itself, and it is essential that this conflict should not be reduced. The growth of a company would suffer if it is organized in such a way as to eliminate this conflict and tension which necessarily arises through the divergent interests of the different dimensions of a company.

In the case of the other two forms of conflict, one arises through interpersonal differences and the other through poor organization. It can now be said that this latter form of conflict arises through inadequate boundary definition; it is conflict over territory. Because the boundaries are obscure, because the structure is not recognized, this conflict is most frequently interpreted at its overt, process level. That is, it is interpreted as a conflict between people, between personalities. Depending on the temperament of the manager in charge, this conflict will be dealt with either by evasion or by suppression. The manager may use various "human relations" methods and so evade the problem, or alternatively the protagonists will be threatened with dire results if they do not "settle their differences." Comparatively few managers are willing or able to go through the delicate and trying process of sorting out the territorial claims of the protagonists.

Sometimes, unwittingly, a manager will even promote this boundary conflict. The manager has a new idea, calls in his subordinates, discusses the idea with them, and sends them away with the exhortation to "sort that out between yourselves, decide who does what, and come back to me with a plan of action." Such a manager feels that he is modern, but he has only abandoned his responsibility, rather than delegating it.

The staff/line theory, and the organization based upon it, was shown to be organizationally unacceptable. It can now be seen that it is unacceptable for other, "psychological" reasons. The staff/line theory is responsible for much territorial conflict. The traditional way of setting up an organization is to provide territories for one group in the company, while denying territory to another. This necessarily sets up a situation in which the unterritoried individuals vie for the territory, and this will necessarily lead to unending conflict within the organization. It has been said that staff personnel, with the best will in the world, often seek to destroy a company. However, it will be seen that *any manager without adequate territory will be forced into conflict in order to establish a territory from which he can act.*

To illustrate the need for clarity at the boundaries, and to show what will happen in the absence of these boundaries, let us suppose that a man "A" were to invite a guest to his house. "A" would do his best to entertain his guest well and get him to feel relaxed and "at home." But suppose during the evening the guest were to let it be known that he felt he *was* at home! An entirely new relationship will ensue. "A" 's problem would no longer be to get his guest to feel at home, but rather to get him out altogether.

This, in a way, is what happens when two managers get together to discuss some particular problem at work. From the outset one would feel that he "owned" the territory and would invite the other in as guest, i.e., as an adviser. After a while, when the guest makes it known that he in fact considers the territory as his, the conflict starts. The homeowner would probably have no difficulty in solving his problem because he could refer to his deed of sale, and, if necessary, to the property lines or property markers. In the case of role invasion, however, it is rarely possible to establish this ownership. The deed titles, that is, the job descriptions, are generally so loosely worded that they are of little or no value in settling disputes. No attention is given to fixing adequate property markers, that is, decision points. It is, therefore, impossible to contest ownership at an overt level. In the absence of objective criteria, objective solutions are impossible, and subjective, that is, hidden solutions are sought. The contest is often carried on orally, and one of the ways by which some managers attempt to prove ownership of territory is to speak longer and louder about the subject in hand.

The boundary of a role is created by the decisions that can be made by that role. Managers mark their territorial boundaries by initials or signatures. To define the boundaries of a role it is simply necessary to determine what decisions can be made in that role. However, a boundary cannot be a boundary in isolation. Little purpose is served by simply establishing the decision boundaries of one role. It is also necessary to establish the decision boundaries of roles that juxtapose, and this juxtaposition will be brought about through the interaction of task cycles.

A very useful method for establishing territorial boundaries, or role boundaries, is that of using "decision tables," or "decision structures." A decision table gives the task cycle in question and the decisions that are made in various roles within the company in connection with that task cycle. (See Appendix I for an example of a decision table.)

The capacity a person has should match the territory he has. This, too, is given support from ethologists' studies, in particular from studies which led to a particular form of forest conservation. Roebuck vary in the amount of territory they can successfully defend, and therefore the population of roebuck in a forest is in inverse proportion to the quality of the buck. By eliminating lower grade buck the forest conservationist is able to reduce the damage caused to the forest by roebuck.

Territory is not always won, or roles earned. People are promoted over their heads intentionally or by accident, and thus territory is conferred. When territory has been conferred it is necessary for "spurious power" to take the place of genuine power. Genuine power, or authority, is capacity exercised within limits. Spurious power does not recognize limits, and therefore instead of enjoying the freedom that limits adjusted to capacity provide, the possessor of spurious power can only experience license. While freedom gives the power to act according to the circumstances, license is arbitrary. The man with too little territory will be hostile, touchy, and excitable; the man with too much territory will recoil from conflict. He will be dependent upon his host, parasite that he is; he will be dependent upon the one who has conferred the territory upon him. What has been given can be taken away. He would, therefore, act only in the name of his host.

As long as the intention of a man is aligned with the intention of the company, he has the total power of the company to back him and provide him with authority. A man of spurious power, however, has only the intention of retaining command of his territory. This intention cannot be aligned with anything. He is therefore a stranger in the environment and lacks authority. As stated earlier, authority requires limits, and these limits will be provided by the role that has transformation and project cycles. The spurious power of the man whose territory is too great, who cannot cope with the transformation or project cycles, can only be exercised in unstructured situations, in situations dominated by flux. He will generate such flux situations in order to use his power; he will manage by crisis.

If a central will with which intention can be aligned and hierarchy obtained is not manifest, fragmentation of the organization will occur, subgroups will arise, and hostility and argument will break out between these subgroups. The goal of discussion is to reveal the structure inherent in a situation, and it is the adjunct to authority. The goal of argument, on the other hand, is to tear down structure, or to so obscure the structure that it is not capable of providing meaning for a situation. Argument is the handmaiden of spurious power, and it is the principal method for generating flux.

Authority must be shared. It can only exist in interaction with others in authority. Power, however, can be exercised in isolation and is its own satisfaction. The more a man is able to share with others, particularly the more he is able to share an understanding with others, the more authority he can exercise; but the more he exercises power, the more he must break up understanding, reject theory, and turn discussion into argument and rebuff. In the absence of understanding, myths must arise, and these in turn will further obscure understanding.

We spoke earlier about displacement activity. Herring gulls and sticklebacks release energy developed through aggression not by attacking each other, but by adopting an entirely different behavior. Displacement activity frequently occurs when conflict arises between managers. Few managers relish open confrontation or argument at the eyeball-to-eyeball level. The method of forest conservation that we discussed earlier was necessary because roebuck in territorial combat attack not each other but the trees of the enemy. In conflict between managers the attack is made not upon the manager himself, but upon the systems and procedures he has developed. This attack is made by undermining the confidence others have in the manager, in his system, and in his ability. At whatever level of competence a manager who is thus attacked is operating, his effectiveness in the company is reduced considerably, and the company as well as the manager concerned must suffer. For lack of an overt method for satisfactorily solving territorial dispute, a whole company and its systems can be laid waste.

It can be seen now why it was so important to address the problem raised of the relative positions of the stockholder and the employee. As long as it is believed that the stockholder "owns" the company, the problem of territory will not be properly solved. An interesting question, and one that can always be relied upon to provide considerable stimulation to an otherwise dull meeting, is to ask people present: Who "owns" the system under discussion? For example, one may find the planning engineer and the manufacturing manager having an argument. One could ask, "Who owns the production system?" The first answer frequently given is, "The shareholder owns the production system." This reply is simply an attempt to push the question out of sight. If the questioning is continued, it soon becomes fairly obvious that the disputants do not consider the shareholders as owning the production system at all. And it also becomes obvious that the original argument had ownership as its basis. The managers will want to keep the problem hidden because of the impossibility of finding an overt solution.

It is now possible to tie the notion of territory to another notion that psychologists, particularly those who have developed the field theories, have used: the notion of behavior space. *The behavior space of a person is his territory; his territory is his behavior space.*

Neither territory nor behavior space is physical. It is psychological—or better still, phenomenological. Ego could be considered to be introjected territory; territory could be looked upon as projected ego. The value of territory on the evolutionary scale is that it provides the means by which ego is developed. The importance of having a well-structured role is the same as the importance of having a well-structured ego.

Territorial conflicts between men take place at two levels. At a symbolic level the conflict concerns "physical territory." At the real level the conflict concerns "idea territory." *Territorial conflict at this level concerns itself with who owns the idea.* To own an idea is to own the center of a phenomenological territory. To persuade others to accept that idea is to provide the territory with a boundary. Argument is territorial conflict, and the object of the argument is to capture the idea, much in the same way that the object of battle was once to capture the enemy's capital, or the standard of the enemy, the standard being the symbol of what he stands for.

This concern with who owns an idea is a very real one. Many managers are familiar with the ruse of saying to a person they wish to persuade to adopt a particular idea, "that idea of yours is a very interesting one." The idea referred to, of course, is the very one that the manager wishes to have adopted. Writers and scientists are very aware of the territory provided by their particular subject matter. For instance, Carl G. Jung in *Study of the Psychological Foundation of the Trinity,* says, "In proposing to approach this central symbol of Christianity, the trinity, from a psychological point of view, *I realize that I am trespassing on territory that must seem very far removed from psychology*"[17] (author's italics). The question of ownership is frequently resolved on the basis of primogeniture. Scientists are very aware of the need to publish quickly in order to be the first with an idea and so retain ownership.[18]

The struggle to own and control ideas takes on a grim perspective when ideological wars are waged in order to seize or retain this ownership. The Inquisitions of the Roman Catholic Church, the concentration camps of Nazi Germany and of Stalin's Russia, the cultural revolutions of the Chinese Republic, and the witch-hunts of the McCarthy era are all forms of this ideological war—the need to control the "minds" of men, which is the need to establish a territory with a particular idea as a center and the presence of others, who accept the idea, as periphery.

The Hierarchy and the Alpha Complex

The need for territory would appear to be a fact. Quoting Ardrey: "Man has an innate compulsion or instinct to gain and defend territory. It is genetic and irradicable." Some writers, for example, Ashley Montague, have contested this need for territory and have offered opposing evidence.[19] Montague points out that the orangutan and the gorilla are non-territorials. However, in a study remote from concern with territory, a writer says the following: "In all times and places human beings have resisted the idea that they are nowhere for no particular reason and for no particular purpose. They have almost always managed to find somewhere to be and a reason to be there."[20] The act of finding these locations is crucial to human life for "people seem to go to pieces when events force them to contemplate the ultimate nowhere of their lives. Then they act in ways which the majority of mankind would consider inhuman."[21] This search for somewhere to be is the search for the resolution of the internal conflict of centrality and periphery. "Out of this dialogue, in which the universe tells them they are nowhere, and in which they assert their place and responsibility, grows . . . a beautiful poetic expression."[22]

But just as it is important for a man to be *somewhere*, so it is important to be *someone*. Territory is a manifestation of the assertive aspect of man, of his centripetal aspect, of what we have called "me-as-periphery." To be someone is a manifestation of the intensive mode, of the integrative, of the centrifugal, of "me-as-center." The problem of being someone introduces the problem of status, that is, the problem of a place in a hierarchy.

There is a direct relationship between the center and the hierarchy. Mircea Eliade says in his study of the center that "the most widely distributed variant of the center is the cosmic tree situated in the middle of the universe and upholding the three worlds as upon one axis." On his mystical journey to the center, and thence to the highest heaven, a shaman goes by "climbing up the seven or nine notches of the ceremonial birch tree."[23] This notion of the center and value, that is, the place in the hierarchy, was encountered when we considered territory. The central territories of the Uganda cob were the most valuable and presumably "the highest in the cob hierarchy."[24]

The organization hierarchy is much emphasized in the thinking of managers and in the writings of management theorists. The hierarchy has been over-valued, and it has a very limited and even, on occasions, a negative value in doing work. Work is done along the horizontal dimension of a company, and when hierarchic or status considerations enter they are a nuisance rather than a help. However, the hierarchy has a very strong cohesive value and in this lies its organizational as well as its phenomenological value. The hierarchy is particularly emphasized in organizations that are threatened by disintegration. For example, the hierarchy is stressed in an army because an army has to face the prospect of operating in territory that it does not own. This, in turn, would explain why a strict staff/line organization is desirable in an army, because the "line" is a hierarchic term.

From the studies we have done on the center and periphery, the reason for this cohesiveness can be understood. If a territory is shared, the problem of center and periphery remains unsolved. Territory, because it is shared, no longer acts as a neutralizing agent to the basic polarity. An alternative solution must be found, and this alternative is found in the hierarchy. As one ascends the hierarchy one approaches the center—as one descends the hierarchy, one approaches the periphery. The hierarchy does through the vertical dimension what territory does along the horizontal dimension.

The distance between levels within a hierarchy, however, must be perceptible to the members. If this distance is not perceptible, "half-rank" positions arise. The hierarchy in this case will no longer be able to neutralize the conflict of center and periphery. The two members who ostensibly are superior and subordinate on the hierarchy will, in fact, become colleagues. The higher member will then become a center without a periphery, while the lower member will become a periphery without a center. This will lead each to seek an alternative superior or subordinate, and thereby the structure will be severely threatened. The subordinate will tend to bypass the superior, or the superior will attempt to bypass the subordinate. These two members will find to an increasing degree that they either avoid each other completely or will share a single role. If the latter is the case, territorial conflict will break out. A similar phenomenon is found among animals and is reported by Lorenz: "All social animals are 'status seekers,' hence there is always particularly high tension between individuals who hold immediately adjoining positions in the ranking order; conversely this tension diminishes the further apart these two animals are in rank."[25]

Members at the higher level of the hierarchy generally feel superior to those at the lower levels. Members at lower levels normally accede to the superiority of those at the higher levels, provided that this superiority can be perceived. Men have a strong sense of equity or social justice and the normal man is "committed to achieving what he judges to be his proper place in society and to taking part in social arrangements which provide the proper place for him and for everyone else. He is aware of the difference between himself and others and can judge in what respect others may be more or less competent than himself. In the absence of this sense of difference, of equity and justice, the individual is disturbed by feelings of omnipotence, or by the opposite, impotence and self-depreciation."[26]

It is worth showing how the understanding of center/periphery will help us understand this strange phenomenon wherein simply by ascending the hierarchy, a person will acquire superiority and why it is that this superiority is often generalized and not simply confined to a specific expertise. In order for a lower member to demonstrate his superiority to a higher member, he would have to adopt the center position for the time being. This would restimulate the basic polarity that the hierarchy was designed to neutralize. The hostility generated toward lower members of the hierarchy in their attempts to break through to higher levels is the projection of the basic anxiety generated by the center/periphery polarity.

Members of the higher level repay lower level members for accepting their position in the hierarchy by defending the lower level members. Higher members will normally respect the lower hierarchy and if any form of discipline is necessary, will defer to the appropriate member at the appropriate level of the hierarchy. A member, therefore, who does not respect the superiority of higher members of the hierarchy, and by his actions makes this known, finds himself without the protection and becomes subject to the attack of any members at any level in the hierarchy. Because of the tendency to seek scapegoats, an undefended member frequently can become the scapegoat of the group and thus be driven out entirely. This could be the lot of the manager who engages in entrepreneurial work, which explains the paradoxical behavior in companies in which creativity is both sought after and suppressed.

The Pair

Shigeru Kobayashi, a Japanese writer on management, indicated that the pair relationship is to be found fairly widespread in Japanese industry.[27] He says that the pair is the smallest, most primitive sort of team and the easiest to form. The basic pair in nature is the male/female team, or the husband and wife team. Kobayashi says that a pair is a combination of workers whose relations on the job are just like that of a man and his wife in the home. Traditionally, the functional relationship of a male/female unit has been considered as a holon: the female concerned with the internal aspects, with the home, with survival; the male with the external aspects, with the work, with expression and expansion. It may be that this traditional role has been implanted into women and that the women's liberation movement is right in calling it into question—however, it has proved very effective in many cases. Its value in sharing territory is fairly obvious in so far as the female would be oriented toward the center while the male is oriented toward the periphery.

This holon aspect of the pair is also found in wolves when out hunting in packs. It is said that the leader of the pack always has a second in command. This second in command has the function of maintaining internal harmony within the pack, while the function of the leader lies outside the pack—in determining where the pack should go. A similar sort of arrangement very often exists in companies that have both a president and a general manager. The general manager's function is to ensure that the internal working of the company is maintained, while the president's function is to relate the company to the higher system. Sometimes this same holon relationship exists with the chairman and the president. Very often the "not two, not one" characteristic of the holon is well expressed by the organization chart in which both appear within one organization box.[28]

15. THE DILEMMA

When they think about work most people think of something unpleasant, of something hard, perhaps of something to escape from if possible. The French word for work is *travail,* which is derived from the Latin *trepalium,* an instrument of torture having three stakes. The fact of the "hardness" of work is recognized even among those who find work enjoyable. Work is hard not simply because physical energy is expended—many people find mental work much harder than physical work and will avoid it. Unable to sustain the mental effort required, these people will be found walking around the office building, signing forms, entering into discussions, attending meetings, in fact, doing anything but work. Thinking things through is hard work, coming to a decision is hard work, even thinking about work is hard. But why is this? What is it that we mean when we say that mental work is "hard"?

To do mental work it is necessary to face and resolve a dilemma, and it is because of this that work is hard. If there were no dilemma, there would be no mental work, but because there is a dilemma, work is necessary. In this chapter we shall try to explain this more clearly by showing that a recognizable pattern underlies work. This pattern is the pattern of a dilemma. We shall start by giving a concrete example taken from some clerical work that is done in a gas utility.

In this particular gas utility, a clerical role has been set up to answer and deal with customers' telephone requests for service. The role is called "the customer inquiry clerk." The customer inquiry clerk must answer the telephone calls from customers, find out what the customer

wants, and complete a form. This form will cause a serviceman to visit the customer's home to attend to the com-
plaint by servicing the appliance or gas system. When the
customer phones, he or she is put into a "queue" with
other customers who are calling. A recording explains that
the line is busy for the time being and asks the customer to
wait for a short while.

During most of the year, but particularly during the fall
and early winter when furnaces must be cleaned and lit,
there are many customers calling in at the same time, and
the clerk must work as quickly as possible *to get customers
off the line* so that others do not have to wait too long for
service.

On the other hand, the clerk must *keep the customer on
the line* to get all relevant information accurately and to
ensure that a service call is indeed necessary. Many customers call for service unnecessarily—some calls even
come from people who do not have gas appliances. Others
have forgotten to switch on the appliances or have appliances that do not work because the electrical equipment or
fuses have failed. Provided sufficient explanations are
given on how to check the appliances for these problems,
there are a lot of things that the customer can do by himself and so obviate the need for a service call.

A clerk must balance these two alternatives, but this is
not all. The cost of sending a serviceman to a house to
provide service is very high. The clerk is instructed to *send
out as few servicemen as possible* and not to assign a high
priority to the call unless absolutely necessary. The more
service calls and the higher the priority, the greater the
cost.

On the other hand, a utility must serve customers, and
to ensure satisfaction it is sometimes necessary for a clerk
to send out a serviceman even though technically there is
no need for a call to be made. For example, when the
roads are being tarred customers frequently mistake the
smell of tar for the smell of gas and phone the utility to
complain of a gas leak. A clerk getting a number of calls
from the same location will identify the cause and explain

this to the customers. Many will accept the explanation, but a few will insist upon a service call being made. Therefore a clerk has two more alternatives to balance and these are related to the first two.

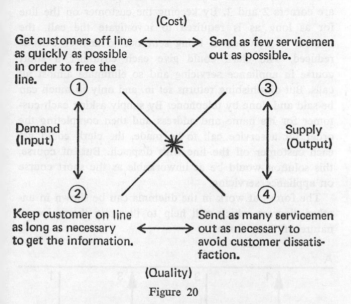

(Cost)

Get customers off line as quickly as possible in order to free the line. ①

Send as few servicemen out as possible. ③

Demand (Input)

Supply (Output)

Keep customer on line as long as necessary to get the information. ②

Send as many servicemen out as necessary to avoid customer dissatisfaction. ④

(Quality)

Figure 20

At corner number 1 we can put the statement, *"Get the customer off the line* as quickly as possible in order to free the line." That is the first requirement.

At corner number 2, we can state, *"Keep the customer on the line* as long as necessary to get sufficient information." This is in direct opposition to number 1.

At corner number 3 we can put the statement, *"Send out as few servicemen as possible* to keep costs down."

At corner number 4, *"Send out as many servicemen as necessary* to avoid customer dissatisfaction." Here again statements 3 and 4 are in opposition.

Corners 1 and 3 are both concerned with costs. The quicker the customer can be dealt with, the fewer clerks are necessary. Corners 2 and 4 are concerned with "quality." These two criteria—cost and quality—form the basic limits of discretion by which results are obtained and work gets done.

However, corners 1 and 4 are complementary and so are corners 2 and 3. By keeping the customer on the line for as long as is required to investigate the call, the number of servicemen being sent out to answer calls is reduced. The clerk could give each customer a short course in appliance servicing and so eliminate almost all calls. But diminishing returns set in, and only so much can be said and done by telephone. By simply asking each customer for his name and address and then completing the order for a service call to be made, the clerk could get each customer off the line with dispatch. But, of course, this solution would be as unworkable as the short course on appliance servicing.

The forces at work in the dilemma can be shown in another diagram which will help to illustrate the universal nature of these forces:

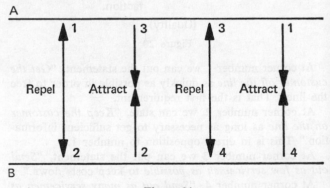

Figure 21

Further understanding of these forces is possible by remembering what we have said about the two tendencies at work within a holon. The first two horns of the dilemma, 1 and 2, are concerned with the internal, integrative aspect of the holon; the second two horns, 3 and 4, are concerned with the external, assertive aspect of the holon. Corners 1 and 2 are concerned with *input or demand,* and corners 3 and 4 with *output or supply.* The opposition between the integrative aspects, 1 and 2, and the assertive aspects, 3 and 4, becomes very apparent if the customer inquiry clerks report to one supervisor and the servicemen to another.

Corners 1 and 3 form the *cost* or integrative aspects and corners 2 and 4 the assertive aspects, or *quality,* of this same system seen as a holon. This time the system is viewed from the point of view of structure; earlier it was viewed from the point of view of process. The system can therefore be illustrated thus:

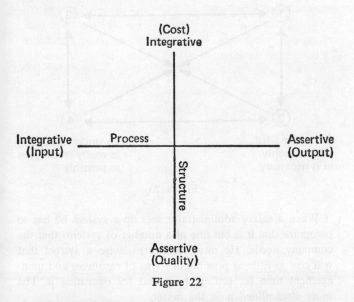

Figure 22

A complete picture has now been given of the tensions at work within the customer inquiry system between the time the clerk says, "Good morning, can I help you?" to when she says, "Thank you very much, good day." In other words, there is a continuous cycle: tension, no tension, tension, no tension; or dilemma, absence of dilemma, dilemma, absence of dilemma.

Let us now take another example of a dilemma, this time an administrative system dilemma. Let us suppose that a salary administrator is asked to set up a salary administration system. This time the following forces will be seen to exist:

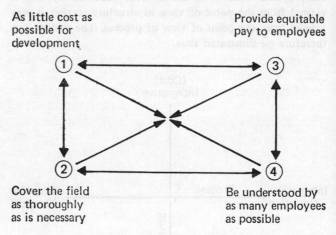

As little cost as possible for development

Provide equitable pay to employees

Cover the field as thoroughly as is necessary

Be understood by as many employees as possible

Figure 23

When a salary administrator sets up a system he has to recognize that it is but one of a number of systems that the company needs. He must therefore devise a system that will cost as little as possible in terms of resources and management time for setting it up and for operating it. The more streamlined it is, the better.

On the other hand, the salary administration system must be as complete as possible; all relevant jobs must be included. For example, if the system is designed for clerical employees, it is unwise to leave out some clerical jobs simply because of the difficulty of including them in the study. Furthermore, all relevant facts must be collected about all the jobs that are involved, and again it would be unwise to deliberately omit relevant facts because of the difficulty or cost of collecting them.

There is, therefore, an antagonism between these two considerations—the same antagonism that we encountered in the earlier example. The more complete the system, the higher the cost is likely to be. The simpler the system, the more likely it is that something will be left out.

In addition, the system must be designed so that it gives satisfaction to those whose salaries are governed by it. One of the requirements of these people is that the salaries are administered equitably, the other is that they understand the system; that is, equity is perceived as such. However, these two requirements are in conflict. Equity is obtained by ensuring that different levels of work are rewarded by correspondingly different levels of pay. Complete equity would prevail when each role had found its exact position in a pay hierarchy. Ideally, this would require a different level of pay for each role. But to explain to an employee why his salary is paid at one level and a colleague's at a slightly different level when the difference between the two roles is barely perceptible is a difficult problem. This problem of explanation is also highlighted when it is remembered that there is always a borderline case whenever one tries to divide a continuum into segments.

Equality is easier to talk about than equity—people understand equality better than equity. Unions have a tendency to want to erode pay differentials as it is easier to communicate equality to the rank and file. The same reason explains why dollars and cents rather than percentage increases are discussed. Dollar and cent increases tend toward equality; percentage increases tend toward equity. Equity, therefore, tends toward one grade for each job, while equality tends toward one grade for all jobs. Again this is a conflict.

Thus, in the illustration of this system (Figure 23), corners 1 and 2 are in opposition and so are corners 3 and 4. Corners 1 and 4, however, are complementary. The less complex the system, the easier it is to communicate. In fact, people often say, "Let's keep it simple," meaning "Let's make it easy to communicate." Corners 2 and 3 are complementary. The more complete and thorough, the greater the chance of equity being reached.

Furthermore, there are two internal aspects concerned with the system and two external aspects concerned with acceptance of the system: the first two concern the make-up of the system, the second two, the reception that others give it. (A full set of salary administration dilemmas is given in Appendix II.)

The Basic Dilemma

In the opening paragraph of this chapter I said that all mental work is concerned with the resolution of the dilemma. Can the insights that were gained from the study of the job of the customer inquiry clerk and the job of setting up a salary administration system be extended to become a general principle related to all jobs? If so, one would get a paradigm that could be used as a means of identifying the particular dilemma underlying any particular work. This would make the dilemma conscious. At present a manager must deal with the dilemma at an unconscious, and therefore inarticulate, level. The solutions he comes to may be correct, but because they are inarticulate they cannot be adequately communicated, nor, often, are they as simple as they could be if they were exposed to the light of conscious reason.

To assist in the development of this common structure, we must refer to some points already discussed. A theory, organization, or system could be judged by reference to four criteria: simplicity, completeness, pragmatism, and communicability. These can be related to our paradigm in the following way:

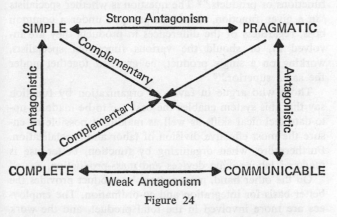

Figure 24

Let us consider an organization to be a system that must be simple, complete, pragmatic, and communicable, and then let us see how it improves our understanding of the problem of organization and the nature of the dilemma.

Organization is simple when there is no overlap between positions and therefore no redundancy in the system. Organization is complete when all work that should be done is done. The more complete the organization, the more complex it is likely to be. The more complexity, the greater the chance of territorial conflict. The simpler the organization, the less chances of conflict, but the greater the chances of something being left undone.

What we have said can be illustrated by the product-function opposition, which is a common problem encountered in organization. A basic problem that arises in organization is whether delegation of work should be made in terms of the "product" or the "function." "The dilemma of product versus function is by no means new; managers have been facing the same basic question for decades."[1] "Corporations, especially manufacturers, have long wrestled with the problem of how to structure their organizations to enable employees, particularly specialists, to do their jobs with maximum efficiency and productivity. One perplexing issue has been whether to organize around functions or products."[2] The question is whether specialists "in a given function, should be grouped under a common boss, regardless of the differences in products they are involved in, or should the various functional specialists, working on a single product, be grouped together under the same superior."[3]

Those who argue in favor of organization by function say that this system enables the best use to be made of up-to-date technical skills as well as making it possible to ensure the most effective division of labor and specialization. Furthermore, when organizing by function, better use is made of labor-saving devices and mass-production.

On the other hand, management by product provides the better basis for integration and co-ordination. The employees are more involved in the total product, and the work they do is more "enriching." Thus, it is likely to create greater challenge as the work is more personalized, calling forth greater commitment.

A. H. Walker and J. W. Lorsche, quoted above, considered specialization (or "differentiation" as they would call it) and "integration" as two horns of a dilemma. Integration corresponds to what we have referred to as simplicity, and differentiation corresponds to completeness. By differentiating roles, the chances of the field being covered completely is increased; by concentrating upon integration, a manager ensures that the system will remain unified and simple. Differentiation generates conflict, but also challenge. Integration provides teamwork, but can lead to complacency. Lorsche says in another article, "The issues involved are so complex that many managers oscillate between these two choices or try to effect some compromise between them."[4] This oscillation approximates the solution arrived at by Bruno's ass who, fixed exactly midway between two bales of hay, starved to death. Many managers, partially aware of the dilemma and wanting the best of both worlds, are unwilling to relinquish either horn and unable to accept both, and so end up with neither.

In the drive toward completeness many companies have become increasingly differentiated, which increases the tendency for roles to become isolated. To overcome the problems created by this isolation, meetings are often conducted and an attempt is made to arrive at joint decisions. In the light of our conclusions about territory it will be seen that an insistence upon joint decisions will give results not unlike the results the Soviets got by insisting upon collective farming. The care and concern that arises out of private ownership is lost. But, on the other hand, the "prima donna" complex that exclusive ownership of territory bestows can be a devastating influence within a company, and joint decision making is one way to avoid this complex.

The more unified a system, the simpler and more integrated it is, and therefore in terms of the two aspects of the holon, simplicity serves the survival or integrative mode. To be complete an organization must constantly reach out into untried fields, and therefore the completeness mode corresponds to the self-assertive mode. But, as we saw with the clerical role, corners 1 and 2 of the dilemma paradigm represent the integrative mode of the holon viewed along the process dimension. Thus, simplicity and completeness concern the way that roles, tasks, operations, and functions are delegated. They are concerned with the *efficiency* of the system. Corners 3 and 4, representing the pragmatic and communication aspects, form the assertive mode and concern the output of these roles, the self-transcendent aspect of the holon, and the *effectiveness* of the system.

The pragmatic criterion—the criterion of "does it work?"—is the one most often invoked by managers when judging an organization. However, it is not enough that a system accomplish work. It must be used by people and therefore has to be communicated to and accepted by them. These two criteria, the pragmatic and communicable, are in opposition. To their dismay, many people have discovered this when, having developed a completely workable way to solve a problem, they find that the higher system refuses to accept the solution because the solution does not conform to its particular way of seeing the world. *That* a system is workable is sometimes the very reason for its rejection. "Every new and good thing is liable to seem eccentric and perhaps dangerous at first glimpse, perhaps more than what is really eccentric, really irrelevant to life."[5]

Sometimes a manager must make up his mind whether to aim at getting results or getting acceptance, and many a manager has forced this dilemma upon his subordinates. Often a manager will do what is easily and readily acceptable even though he knows it will produce no worthwhile result. "What does it matter if the grass does not grow as long as it is green."

There are instruments in many workmen's tool kits that are designed to make work easier or more effective but are never used because the men do not understand how to use them. The instruments are "pragmatic" but not "communicable." This is true also of many systems developed within an organization as well as of organizations themselves.

The paradigm that we have given, therefore, shows that the structure of the dilemma underlying work is complex and cannot be dealt with by ordinary logic. Indeed, the value of logic is to break open the dilemma and allow one to proceed as though its two horns were simply opposites. But the dilemma is not one, not two; the opposition within the dilemma makes it behave as though it were two, but its concreteness, its reality, resides in its unity. To break it into two is to destroy its very potential.

The dilemma, or its intellectual counterpart the paradox, is, as C. G. Jung points out, essential if one is to describe a complete system. "Oddly enough, the paradox is one of our most valuable spiritual possessions, while uniformity of meaning is a sign of weakness. Hence a religion becomes inwardly impoverished when it loses or reduces its paradoxes; but their multiplication enriches because only the paradox comes anywhere near to comprehending the fullness of life. Non-ambiguity and non-contradiction are one-sided and thus unsuited to express the incomprehensible."[6]

The dilemma not only underlies work, but all human activity.[7] The exposition of the dilemma or the paradox is very complicated and is often very difficult to grasp. But because it leads one to the very core of work itself—to the difficulty of work—and even to the very core of life, it cannot be neglected. Again quoting Jung: "Scientific integrity forbids all simplification of situations that are not simple, as is obviously the case here. The pattern of relationship is simple enough, but, when it comes to a detailed description in any case it is extremely difficult to see from which angle it is being described and what aspect we are describing."[8]

This chapter began with an implied question: "What is it that makes work difficult?" We have come to the conclusion that the difficulty of work resides in the tension generated by the dilemma. Nevertheless, it has been stressed that people enjoy work and that failure to find work of sufficient challenge causes a deterioration in the personality. It would appear that there is a contradiction in these two statements because one of the more obvious aspects about people is that they seem to want to get rid of tension; to eliminate tension from themselves. The mind could even be considered to be a tension-reduction system.

If, however, we were to regard the mind as *only* a tension-reduction system, we should find forms of behavior that are impossible for us to understand. For example, why do people go to see horror movies; in fact, why do people go to see any film or play at all? A good drama goes through a steady build-up of tension; Shakespeare, for example, would build up tension and then, by employing humor, release some of it, only so that more tension could be built up subsequently. In most good plays there are three or four peaks of tension. At the height of tension a synthesis is realized and a catharsis or release of tension results.

There appear to be two tendencies at work in people, and the mind appears to be a tension-induction/reduction system. Each person has a certain tension tolerance, and his aim would be to match his tolerance of tension to the work at hand. We tend to reduce the level of work to our level of tolerance if the tension is too high, or on the other hand, we tend to increase the level of tension if it is too low. At a particular time one feels underworked, and as a consequence looks around for more to do. More and more is found until the feeling comes about that one is over-worked, and as a consequence one starts letting go of more and more work until the feeling of being underworked recurs. Observing oneself over a period of several months, it will be found that a fairly regular cycle of over-work/underwork is experienced. Parkinson's law expressed half of this cycle while the Peter principle expresses the other half.

There seems to be a need for tension in the system, but tension under control. As long as there is tension under control, life is interesting. It is when tension exceeds the point of tolerance that life becomes unbearable. Many people leave one job for another because they feel that the earlier job offers too little challenge, and challenge is that which induces tension in the system. Boredom is one of the worst of all experiences, and boredom arises when a plateau has been reached and there is no tension in the system anymore.

The work situation is a creation that has great psychological value. Through work man is able to escape the effects of the dilemma by projecting it into the work situation. In a well-organized situation the dilemma is, as it were, caged, and the man is able to enjoy its power without seemingly paying its price. Work is not the invention of Western man; our contribution has been to deify work. Industrial work is modern man's answer to a religiousless society. In past societies religion provided the source of man's work, and through spiritual work religion

showed man how to go beyond the dilemma. The Mandala
of the Buddhists and the Cross of the Christians can be
seen to be symbols of the conflicting forces to which man
is subject and the degree of suffering that these forces can
create. Zen, more than any other spiritual discipline, in-
vites man to seek the heart of the primordial dilemma, to
open himself to its implications and to finally resolve the
dilemma in a way that does not destroy its potential.

16. IDEA AND THE FOUR CRITERIA

We can now define capacity as the potential to create ideas in order to resolve dilemmas in such a way that growth, expansion, and self-regulation take place. The notion of idea is a very important one throughout our study. We have said that Will is divided against itself, and that this gives rise to perception and behavior, which together constitute work, and that the outcome of work is a product. A product is a means by which the opposing tendencies of a company can be reconciled. The tendencies toward survival and assertion as well as the structural and process tendencies are reconciled in the product—an idea in a form with a demand. We must, therefore, give some more attention to what an idea is, and we shall find this no less perplexing than the problem of trying to explore the nature of the basic polarity. It is said, "It is more difficult to make truth known than it is to discover truth. Furthermore, as the propositions one is making become more general, the complications involved in bringing out the meaning increase and so do the difficulties in being precise."[1] In the notions of the basic polarity, the dilemma, and the idea, we are addressing the most general of notions. Furthermore, we are attempting to do this in a practical way, a way that will enable us to address more meaningfully the very real problems of work and organization.

Although it is important, very little mention is made in management literature of the notion of "idea." As we have already said, managers in the modern Western world are severely hampered in gaining an understanding of what is meant by idea, principally because of the dominance of the rationalistic, positive approach. This is particularly true in America where behaviorism, which sets narrow and artificial limitations upon what is acceptable as data, flourishes. The behaviorists have failed to confront the dilemma and have opted in favor of being bound by technical rules limited in vision, being devoid of personal involvement, and being oriented to careers.[2] By studying behavior rather than an indefinable psyche, an objectivity, albeit a pseudo objectivity, was given to the observations of scientists interested in understanding human beings. But behavior, as we have already shown, is only one pole of the polarity providing the dynamics in human nature. The most serious consequence of this emphasis on behavior is the decline in popularity of such words as "consciousness," "will," "soul," etc., and the decline in popularity of the notion of idea.

However, without this notion of idea one cannot even broach the subject of creativity or work, as the literature of behaviorism shows. How, for example, does the behaviorist believe that we obtain a new creation such as a poem, an essay, a management report, or a new practice or procedure in a company? "We get them by manipulating words, shifting them about until a new pattern is hit upon. . . . How do you suppose that Patou builds a new gown? Has he any picture in his mind of what the gown is to look like when it is finished? He has not. . . . He calls his model in, picks up a piece of silk, throws it around her, he pulls it in here and pulls it out there. . . . He manipulates the material until it takes on the semblance of a dress. . . . Not until the creation aroused admiration and commendation, both his own and others, would manipulation be completed—the equivalent of a rat's finding food. . . . The painter plies his trade in the same way, nor can the poet boast of any other,"[3] nor, presumably, can the manager.

According to J. B. Watson, from whom the above quotation came, von Braun presumably took some metal, punched it here and bored it there, and not until it was universally admired did he have it sent to the moon as a rocket.

One thing with which we can agree with the behaviorists is that it is very unlikely that Patou, von Braun, or any manager has a picture or image in his mind when he works. Instead he has an idea, an idea that guides him to his destination, to his product. This is then put in contest with other ideas and with the environment to learn whether it is fit enough to survive.

An idea is immediately given. It reveals relations between phenomena, and it is therefore more immediate than phenomena. It is prior to phenomena. Not prior in time, but prior in level. Fact expresses relations between phenomena. Fact is the crystallization of that nexus of relations perceived through the idea. Idea and fact are the two dimensions of a holon. In spite of, indeed because of, its immediacy, it is difficult to say what is meant by the word "idea." This difficulty comes not from a lack of technical competence, but because it arises from pure intuition and not from deduction.

We cannot, however, retreat from the task of trying to make clear the meaning of the term "idea." Idea is that which reconciles the dilemma, and it is that out of which the product grows. Therefore, it is the seed of the company. To fail to understand "idea" would be to fail to understand the very meaning of work, organization, or a company. In the following examples I will illustrate various aspects of "idea" and will show that the idea-fact holon is not a "thing" but an operation, an act of Will. Furthermore, it is an operation having characteristics with which we are already familiar.

The Hidden Man

An idea reveals relations between phenomena, the prime stuff of experience. Technically, a phenomenon is *"that which shows itself in itself,* the manifest."[4] A field of phenomena is that which appears. Out of that which appears, experience is derived through structure imposed by the idea. Prime phenomena, unstructured phenomena, are unknown to us. Phenomena are always offered within a framework of some kind, and chaos is relative. Figure 25[5]

Figure 25

is a field of phenomena. To all intents and purposes it is a two-dimensional field. Those who see this field for the first time generally agree that it has no definite form, that it is a relative chaos, that it is a random display of irregular black-and-white forms.

The field is best structured by the *idea* of a man, or rather the idea of the head and torso of a man. (It is important to notice that the field has a *best* structure, a theme to which we shall return later in our study.) This idea can structure the field with such clarity that it is possible for a discussion to take place between two people about the field. It could be contended that the picture is that of a bearded man, but such a contention simply creates confusion and blankness in most people who have not perceived the torso or face in the field.

It is necessary to *work* in order to see the face. By this work the field of phenomena, which is a black-and-white confusion, is changed into a face. The medium through which the change is brought about is the idea. The idea does not exist in the phenomena. If it did, all people would readily perceive the face. Phenomena is quite passive. The idea will arise as a consequence of the need to find order in chaos, to structure what is otherwise unstructured, to find a pattern.

In perceiving chaos there is confusion and tension. When order has been put into chaos, there is a release from tension. It has been said that people who have been blind from birth and who subsequently undergo an operation to have their sight restored find that the perceptual confusion that greets them is so great, and the work involved in learning how to structure this perceptual confusion so difficult, that many wish they were blind once more.

Those who struggle to structure the field notice that after a while they begin to feel tense, even somewhat irritated. Once they see the face, however, they experience considerable relief, a feeling of satisfaction; some have a feeling of surprise and others even a feeling of amusement when the face becomes clear.

The face does not appear in stages. *It appears complete, whole, or it does not appear at all.* Observing others working, struggling to see the face, one can identify immediately when they have accomplished the work, when they have seen the face. A sudden change occurs in them. It is essential that some tension should build up in order to do this work adequately. In any creative work tension is necessary, but the tension must be well contained. In this instance, the two dimensional framework of the field of phenomena acts as an adequate container for the energy built up by the work.

The field that we are shown in Figure 25 is very similar to the field of phenomena that we encounter in our everyday life. However, everyday life has more dimensions and is therefore much more complex. Nevertheless, we are constantly called upon to structure the field of our everyday life in such a way to overcome the confusions and tensions brought about by lack of order. Furthermore, with the particular field that we are given in Figure 25 there is but one adequate way to structure it in order to bring about optimum interaction with others—as shown below. Later examples will show that this is not always the case.

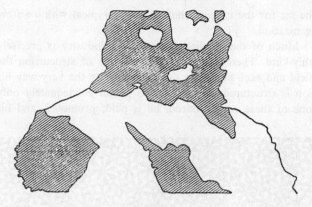

Figure 26

Recall the earlier illustration of the vase/two faces (Figure 15). It represents another two-dimensional field. In that illustration the field is more readily structured; less struggle is necessary to acquire a satisfying structure. However, a new problem arises: the field of phenomena can be structured in two entirely different ways; the field is *multistable*. Either two faces or a vase can be seen; both cannot be seen simultaneously. "Some exponents of the older psychology have maintained that in such instances one figure is noticed while the other goes unnoticed for the time being. Gestalt psychologists reject this approach,"[6] and so affirm the importance of structuring the field.

With the picture of the hidden man, the problem was one of "what must be included in the structure?" In Figure 15 the problem is rather "what should be rejected?" Let us suppose that this picture were shown to two men in a company by their manager and suppose that the manager were to say, "I want you two to get together to write a story about what you see on the card. If you do it well, I shall give you more money, promotion, prestige, and I shall help you reinforce your self-esteem considerably. But I only want one theme in the story." If one of the men were to see a vase and the other to see two faces, the stage would be set for the type of conflict that is typical within an organization.

Much of the conflict that arises in industry is precisely this kind. There are a number of ways of structuring the field and each person in the company, by the very way his job is structured, is expected to perceive adequately only one of these ways. Indeed, he is paid, promoted, and his

Figure 27

self-esteem is reinforced to the extent that he is able to exploit that particular way.

Patterns

Figure 27 illustrates another aspect of "idea." At first glance the field is seen to be a black-and-white field with some regularity. Normally most people see first the wind-mill-shaped patterns dispersed about the field. If one studies the field further, however, other patterns begin to appear, and the longer the field is studied the more intricate the patterns become. The "mind" does not simply accept a chaotic field, but seeks instead to structure this field.[7] Figure 27 shows that in order to bring as much of the field as possible into a single grasp, patterns are made increasingly complex. Closer inspection of what is done will show that the mind builds up patterns, and, when as much of the phenomena has been integrated within that pattern or idea as can be, it will release the idea, return the field to its original state of chaos, then build up new patterns, new ideas, in the hope of integrating even more phenomena within a single grasp. As the pattern becomes more complex, the structure becomes more unstable, having a greater tendency toward disintegration. The release of the pattern and the return to chaos is a retrogressive step, *"un reculer pour mieux sauter."*[8]

The next two illustrations give further evidence of the tendency of the mind to simplify the field by perceiving a pattern and to include as much of the field as possible. But they also show the problems encountered by the mind when it attempts to express the idea; that is, relate the idea or pattern to a higher system in a meaningful way.

The Three Men

The three previous examples showed the tendency of the mind to preserve as much as possible of the field. Figure 28[9] shows the same tendency. It also shows another tendency which is that of relating what is being perceived to a

Figure 28

higher system represented by experience. Experience is the way in which we sum up the totality of previous perceptions. A present perception is both modified by experience and in turn modifies experience.

In this picture of the three men it seems that one is very much larger than the other two. Indeed many people have to measure the three men to assure themselves that the figures are in fact the same size. The mind attempts to integrate the converging lines with the figures by accepting the lines as perspective.

The Three Triangles

Figure 29

This picture of three triangles[10] illustrates yet another tendency, the tendency to simplify toward meaning. First read the words in each triangle quite quickly. Do this several times and a striking fact will suddenly appear: A word is duplicated in each triangle! Most people will read what is in the triangle several times before this fact emerges. This simple demonstration shows the tendency of the mind to simplify as much as possible, to eliminate unnecessary elements in order to obtain a satisfactory whole, satisfactory in relation to the higher system. This time the higher system is the meaning of the phrase. In other words, the simplification of the phrases as subsystems enables them to participate more readily within the system of language. The meaning of the subsystem is therefore toward the simplification of the system.

The Tuning Fork

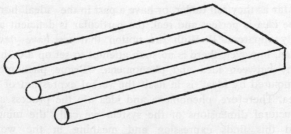

Figure 30

One final picture will show what we already know: The "mind" can run into very real difficulties when it attempts to both simplify and be complete. By looking at this picture from one end or the other, the figure is a simple whole. But the figure itself contains a contradiction. The picture presents a dilemma. The "mind" finds it as satisfactory to accept completeness as it does simplicity, and equally unsatisfactory to sacrifice either.

In attempting to describe the way people structure a field we have used the word "mind," a term likely to cause some difficulties. "Mind" is often considered to be a receptacle of experience, and therefore opposed to experience. "Mind" is looked upon, perhaps, as a cup that is filled, or a slate that is written upon. No such meaning is to be ascribed to the word "mind" as it is now being used. As with the term "organization," "mind" has three meanings: It is an operation, a structure, and a process. As an operation, "mind" and "idea" are synonymous. As a structure, "mind" is the pattern arising out of the idea-fact holons within a common presence. As a process, it is the ebb and flow of structured phenomena.

It is also important to distinguish between the notion of idea that we are presenting and the Platonic "ideal." Plato postulated an ideal world populated by archetypal images, or ideas, which gave form to the real world. "Somewhere or other there is an 'ideal horse,' the horse as such, unique and unchanging . . . Particular horses are what they are in so far as they fall under, or have a part in the 'ideal' horse. The idea is perfect and real, the particular is deficient and only apparent."[11] With the notion that we have developed, however, there is no such attempt to set up a dichotomy between idea and phenomena. "Prime phenomena structured by idea" is in itself the verbal expression of an idea. Therefore, phenomena and idea are the process and structural dimensions of the system we call "the mind," and this finds expression and meaning in the world through language and behavior.

A further distinction should be made between idea and image: an image is a product of the functional aspect of mind, whereas idea is a perception of will. Image, therefore, is one way that idea finds expression through fact.

Idea and the Four Criteria

In Chapter 15 we developed a common structure for the dilemma based upon four criteria. We saw that the criteria of simplicity and completeness were in opposition, as were the criteria of pragmatism and communicability; while simplicity and completeness formed one face of a holon, pragmatism and communicability formed the other. Now we shall take our study one step further to show that these four criteria can be described better as operations of Will, and we can make the following proposition: Will in its operation manifests as center and periphery, and the tension generated as a consequence gives rise to limitations. *These limitations acting as operations can also be understood as operations leading to the simple, complete, pragmatic, and communicable. Within these limitations all creativity and therefore growth, including evolution, occurs.* As the primary manifestation of will has been said to be the perception of an idea and its expression as fact, we must show that these four criteria can be used as operations leading to the idea/fact holon. This will show that the dilemma is at the very core of being and is a direct result of the center-periphery polarity. It will also show that the very experience of reality as *real* comes from the dilemma.

Simplicity and Completeness

Each of the diagrammatic illustrations given earlier in this chapter shows the tendency toward simplicity. There is not "really" a hidden face, there are "just" black-and-white areas. The simplest way to view these black-and-white areas is to see it as a face. This simplest way unifies many of the phenomena so that they can be grasped in a single idea. But there is also a tendency toward completeness that makes the face difficult to see. Because of the reluctance to disregard about a third of the phenomena, some people have difficulty seeing the face. When some of the extra phenomena are eliminated through a sketch, as in Figure 26, this difficulty no longer exists.

With the ambiguous picture, the problem of simplicity is not very great. The vase and two faces are clearly defined. However, the problem of completeness is increased as one of the two "solutions" must be rejected; furthermore, it is as comfortable to reject the black as it is to reject the white. It is this unwillingness to reject either the white or the black that brings about the alternation. An article in

Scientific American suggested that this alternation arises through fatigue in the neural structures: "The alternative aspects of the figure are represented by activity in different neural structures, and when one such structure becomes 'fatigued,' or satiated or adapted, it gives way to another that is fresher and more excitable."[12] Although there may be a neural limit beyond which one cannot hold a figure without it changing into its opposite, nevertheless an alternation is often induced before this limit is reached, and this alternation is explained by the need for completeness, by the need to integrate the whole field.

However, this alternation between two equally attractive alternatives is well known to us all. It is also expressed in the need to avoid waste. The more unified the mind becomes, the greater the need for completeness. Because of the reluctance to waste, the dilemma is created. Situations eventually arise where one end or the other of the stick can be had, but not both. The illustration of the tuning fork (Figure 30) shows this very well. There is a corollary to this which is that one will waste to the extent that one is unable to tolerate the dilemma. Thus, the exponents of the view that a company is in business to make a profit, the exponents of the univalent view designed to reduce the level of dilemma, are in fact waste generators. This is the antithesis to making a profit.

In our illustrations the need for simplicity and completeness is realized through the perception of structure having an increasingly higher level of structure. The tension between the simple and complete poles is expressed through increasing instability of the pattern. Another way in which the opposing tendencies of simplicity and completeness are expressed is through repetition of identical structures. This is a sacrifice of total unification, but it enables an attainment of a higher order of completeness.

According to André Lamouche, the principle of simplicity "plays a role of screen and intellectual catalyst, analogous to that played by the principle of identity in Aristotelian times and in the centuries that followed."[13] He points out that although there is no notion that has been invoked more often by scholars, no one has defined this term precisely. This same notion of simplicity has also been invoked by the Gestalt psychologists who have been responsible for much research into perception: "One perceives the 'best' figure that is consistent with a given image. For practical purposes, 'best' may be taken to mean 'simplest.'"

There is no prior logic to which Will appeals when selecting the simple and complete; logic is derived from this striving. *Simplicity is an operation;* it is that which is done and not a concept or that which is used in thinking. The striving to simplify phenomena while striving for completeness is that operation by which perception is achieved. Idea is itself a holon which arises out of the Will and its inner contradiction of center and periphery.

The Pragmatic and Communicable

An idea is expressed either as behavior or as fact. At this point we are interested in exploring the idea/fact holon, although it is important to see that an idea does not have to be expressed as a fact. The simplest expression of the idea/fact holon is, "This is that": "This" is the idea,[14] "that" is the fact. "That" is also a holon which is the outcome of the pragmatic and communicable. In other words, fact is the outcome of a special kind of behavior called verbalizing—either overt through talking or writing, or covert in thinking. We pick up one of the illustrations and ask, "What is this?" and we name the illustration by saying this is a vase, a face, a tuning fork, and so on. This need to name things seems basic. In Genesis the first thing that man does is name creation. Some names are taboo in the belief that to name is to control. The basic pragmatic action is naming as this expresses the idea in consciousness and brings it into time. To name also separates things. Naming is an intensive definition of phenomena and is to fact what simplifying is to idea.

The communicable is that which can mesh with the higher system, which, for a fact, is experience. Although naming isolates things, things are not alone. When we ask, "What is this?" we ask also, "How does this fit in with my experience?" This experience is sometimes very loosely structured and at other times highly structured—a scientific theory, for example—but nevertheless new facts must fit in. Science incorporates facts with the higher system through a process of measurement, and measurement is a common denominator of things.

In the picture of the three men (Figure 28) the opposition between the pragmatic and the communicable is brought out. Through the pragmatic operation a fact of three men walking along a road in a tunnel is created; but whoever looks at this feels uncomfortable because the three men are really the same size. Experience also dictates that men are not dwarves and giants. Thus, there is a struggle in our minds between the fact of three men walking along a road and the fact of three men of the same size against a lined background. The first of these alternatives wins because it is also supported by the idea. However, if parallel lines are drawn along the hats and feet of the men the opposition between the communicable and pragmatic is heightened.

While the pragmatic is associated with naming things, the communicable is associated with the meaning of things, and as the pragmatic and communicable are in opposition, it will not be surprising to learn that two opposing systems of logic are derived from the pragmatic and the communicable. These two are Aristotelian logic and the logic of the general semanticists. These two logics are clearly in opposition to each other as the founder of general semantics, Alfred Korzybski, makes very clear. A very brief look at these two systems will help in clarifying something of the nature of the opposition between the pragmatic and the communicable.

The word "thing" originally meant a "collection." A thing can be looked upon in two ways—the Aristotelian, in which it is something with properties which themselves have properties; or the general semantic way in which a thing is a point event, a coming together of things which themselves are a coming together of things. By naming something we separate it as figure from ground. When we say this is a vase, the white becomes figure and the black ground. This act of separation grants reality to the figure and the ground is left in limbo; it is not as real. This "reality" that we create by names is the reality of the engineer, and technology is concerned with creating that kind of reality that can be manipulated by technology. General semantics is at pains to clearly separate the name from the "thing." The map, they say, is not the territory. This allows the "thing" to become fluid once more, to mesh easily with the higher system. It can become more readily figure or ground. General semantics means meaning and the non-Aristotelian logic of the semanticists is concerned with the meaning of things rather than the reality of things. Aristotelian logic is the logic of the center: "A is A" makes A a unique, stable, and enduring center. The logic of the semanticists is that of the periphery, the logic of process.

The full dilemma of the idea/fact holon, being itself made up of two holons—a simple/complete and a pragmatic/communicable holon—can only be hinted at by the illustrations and only referred to in a study such as this. It could be more clearly explored in a study of art or literature. Poetry is the art form concerned with expressing ideas through facts while retaining the simplicity, fullness, existence, and togetherness of a situation. As Zen is that discipline most concerned with coming to terms with the dilemma, it is not surprising that it would have inspired a poetic art form that is unique. It is called the *haiku* and allows but seventeen syllables with which to express an idea. The perception of the idea is the basis of creativity, and the ever-renewing struggle of the artist arises through the dilemma that is basic to the very act of perceiving. There is a difference between looking and seeing in that in the former the dilemma is passive, while in the latter it is active.

The artist feels the complexity and incompleteness of the current view of the world and seeks to find a simple and more complete view. If he is a true artist, he obeys his medium and accepts the conflict coming from the need for richness of content and elegance of form. Creativity involves a constant risk and a constant sacrifice. The sacrifice is concerned with relinquishing the old, with letting go that which has been established. The risk is that the new may fail to match what is required, and it may fail to communicate.

The established is the conscious, and the conscious is that which has already found expression. The conscious is that from which we derive the structure which provides meaning. The idea is germinated in simplicity and completeness and blooms or is expressed in the conscious—the established—by way of expression and meaning. The idea is therefore *preconscious*. "Consciousness" and "being" are intimately related; therefore, idea is also "pre-being." *Idea is the "eye" of the Will*. The term "eye of the will" is a term that is also given to "attention."

The relationship of perceiving the idea and creativity can also be understood by reference to the work done on creativity by Arthur Koestler. Koestler saw creativity as "the perceiving of a situation or idea in two self-consistent but habitually incompatible frames of reference."[15] Koestler coined the word "bisociation" in order to distinguish between the routine skills of thinking on a single plane and the creative act. We can now see that all perception is the bisociation of the two incompatible frames of reference[16] established by the center-periphery polarity. Furthermore, we can see that Jaques's definition of work applies to the perception and expression of the idea in the idea/fact holon, and therefore employment work is just one manifestation of the creative act of which perception is the prototype.

17. COMMITMENT, CAPACITY, AND ABILITY

Work, we have stated, is the "exercise of discretion within limits to produce a product," and discretion was further defined as capacity in action. But it is necessary to go more deeply into the question of what is meant by discretion. In doing this it will be seen first that "capacity" is different from "ability" to do work, and second that the dimensions of performing work are isomorphic with organization dimensions. Capacity stands to structure as ability stands to process: In both capacity/ability and structure/process the field is held together by commitment.

The idea that "all men are born equal" is basic to our political institutions, but at the same time, our economic institutions are based upon "free enterprise." The philosophical bases of the Western economic institutions are still the *laissez faire* philosophies of Adam Smith and other like-thinking social philosophers of the nineteenth century. *Laissez faire* allows men to compete freely in order that the fittest might survive, and assumes that the fittest will also be able to benefit society the most by providing not only for himself but for others as well. *Laissez faire* and the notion that all men are born equal are two basic premises of Western democracies—and they are contradictory.

In industry it is often believed that those who "rise to the top" do so by some virtue of diligence, self-sacrifice, application, and hard work. For a long time it was believed that if a man were to work hard enough, he was bound to succeed. This myth was based upon the myth of the equality of man. It was said that in Napoleon's army every soldier carried a field marshal's baton in his haversack. But it is apparent that no matter how hard some people may work, they will never rise very high in the management hierarchy. On the other hand, it is quite evident that many men are able to rise through management levels without a great deal of apparent effort, the power politics of organizations notwithstanding.

The equality/non-equality polarity is reconciled by the notion of the holon that we have already developed. Man in his integrative mode is equal in so far as he is unique. In his self-assertive mode, man finds his place in a natural hierarchy.

It is man in his assertive mode that we shall consider. It is important to make this distinction because we must understand that we are by no means considering the totality of man when we consider man as manager. Although there is a great tendency to do so, we must not make the mistake of equating a level on the management hierarchy with a level on the human hierarchy.

What is it that enables one man to go to the head of a company while another finds that a foreman's level is too much for him? Is it simply that one man has more education, the right sort of experience, or more luck than another? It is suggested that the potential for operating at different levels in the organization hierarchy arises out of the *capacity* and *ability* to do work and the *willingness to commit* that capacity and ability within a particular framework. We shall find that each of these three primary dimensions are in themselves complex structures, which we shall explore in some detail. In the end, it will be found that the paradigm given earlier of a company will illustrate exactly the structure of commitment, capacity, and ability.

Commitment

Multifaceted information is received by a person and processed through the perception of ideas into concepts. These concepts are expressed through language and give rise to behavior and feedback in terms of structured experience. This experience is, in its turn, the basis of further information which is structured, processed, and again expressed. Information is, therefore, "digested" and this digesting process is one in which the information is first reduced to its simplest relationships, while at the same time wasting as little of the information as possible. It is then reassimilated within a wider framework, thereby modifying the framework while being subject to it. This digestion is precipitated by a central idea: "I am I?"

"I am I?" is a multistable phenomenon having two mutually exclusive yet mutually dependent sources of origin: me-as-center and me-as-periphery. The stability of this relationship has to be maintained, and this is done through projection. One manifestation of this projection is "need." "I am I?" is the experience of the lack of something and this is what is meant by need.

Each person has a total philosophy of life, a *Weltanschauung*. It is an expression of his basic commitment and the differences in this basic commitment account for the differences in *Weltanschauung*. However, this basic commitment is complex. Therefore, paradoxically, the average man does not have a unified or single "I"; he has a number of independent "I's," each of which in its turn forms a center or focus of will.[1] Each of these arises out of a need or a complex of needs. This multiplicity of I's gives rise to the inauthenticity of man, because an authentic man wills but one thing.[2]

For many years the industrial world has been dominated by the myth of "economic man." It has been believed that man can be understood simply in terms of economic needs. More recently a structure in terms of a hierarchy of needs has been expounded by Maslow, and this hierarchy of needs has gained wide acceptance.[3] Maslow has suggested that there is a range of needs, from physiological through those of security and safety, community, status and recognition, and the need for self-actualization. Ardrey in his studies has suggested a triad of needs: the need for security, the need for stimulation, and the need for identity.

Given that there are both centrifugal and centripetal tendencies present, it would be expected that there would be two corresponding *sets* of needs. The centripetal needs can be regarded as security needs, while the centrifugal needs can be regarded as achievement needs. The three levels of need correspond to the physical, social, and spiritual tendencies of man and there is an appropriate system of needs at each of these levels. The first level concerns the physical in which there is a need for activity, comfort, and sustenance. These needs can be analyzed and further subdivided. For example, the need for sustenance can be broken down into the need for food, air, and impressions.

The second level could be called "social needs" and are the needs for power, prestige, and possessions.[4]

The third level of needs are metaphysical: justice, beauty, and truth. These three have been the basic subjects of philosophy and are recognized as the principal spiritual needs of man. The planes and levels may be diagrammed as in Figure 31.

The interpenetration of needs and levels gives rise to the richness of the personality and to the infinite variety of ways in which the commitment of human beings is focused through needs, leading to different sorts of interaction. For example, uniqueness is sought after at all levels: at the level of truth in the origination of new ideas; at the level of possession through the exclusiveness of possession; at the level of sustenance through the idiosyncrasies of diet.

It is commitment, focused by need, that provides the precipitating point, the point of coalescence, around which our experience is structured, and underlying all of these points of coalescence is the basic structure "I am I?" It is commitment that enables us to play the role of parent, spouse, salary administrator, liberal, philosopher, friend, and so on. It is the extent to which this commitment is congruent in us—the extent to which needs, manifested through various roles, mutually support each other—that our will is unified, that we approach individuality. What we commit ourselves to gives rise to the depth and richness of our lives. It determines how we live with ourselves. The

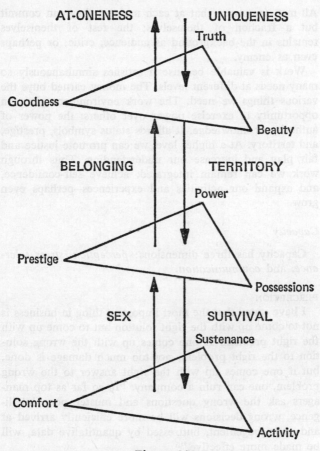

AT-ONENESS

UNIQUENESS

Truth

Goodness

Beauty

BELONGING

TERRITORY

Power

Prestige

Possessions

SEX

SURVIVAL

Sustenance

Comfort

Activity

Figure 31

more unified our basic commitment, the greater our inner coherence.

Each person has a degree of integration within himself, a degree of commitment of which he is capable. This he calls "I." This power to commit changes constantly as circumstances change; it changes both in direction (from centripetal to centrifugal) and in level, as well as in type.

All men are aware that at each moment they can commit but a fraction of themselves; the rest of themselves remains in the background as audience, critic, or perhaps even as enemy.

Work is valuable because it satisfies simultaneously so many needs at different levels. The money earned buys the various things we need. The work environment gives an opportunity to exercise power over others; the power of authority or knowledge. It affords status symbols, prestige, and territory. At a higher level we can promote justice and fair play and increase our understanding. Thus through work we can remain integrated, achieve self-confidence, and expand our activities and experiences—perhaps even grow.

Capacity

Capacity has three dimensions: *perception, stress tolerance,* and *communication.*

PERCEPTION

I have stated that the most important thing in business is not to come up with the right solution but to come up with the right problem. If one comes up with the wrong solution to the right problem, not too much damage is done, but if one comes up with the right answer to the wrong problem, one can ruin a company. "In so far as top managers ask the wrong questions and muster poor intelligence, wrong decisions will be more efficiently arrived at and poor judgement, buttressed by quantitative data, will be made more effective."[5]

There have been many companies that have gone bankrupt because they have been seeking to solve the wrong problems with competence and expertise. A dozen computers working twenty-four hours a day on the wrong problem will simply turn out a mess. The Maginot Line of 1939 was a perfect answer, but the question that was posed was wrong. The French were seeking to solve the problem of how to fight the trench war with none of the inconvenience of trench warfare. The real problem was one of how to fight a mobile war, and the Maginot Line was a disaster. Perceiving a problem is an *intuitive process*,[6] not an intellectual one.

The perception of ideas is best termed a "cosmic-organic" process.[7] Ideas are not ours to own, but simply ours to perceive and express. This is often illustrated by simultaneous discoveries; for example, the discovery of calculus by both Newton and Leibnitz. The notion of the seer as a semidivine being and of the king as an incarnation of the deity, the fear and awe with which the "word" was once held, and the prevalence of magic and superstition all arise out of the recognition that ideas are conceived in the cosmos but perceived in the organism.

A distinction can therefore be made between perception of ideas (or intuition) and the intellectual process of analytical thought. This distinction is not new and many authors and researchers of mental processes have noted these two different ways of "thinking." Oswald Spengler, for example, contrasts them when he states: "The destiny idea demands life experience and not scientific experience, the power of seeing and not that of calculating, depth and not intellect."[8]

This distinction between intuition and analytical thinking is at the root of some critical re-evaluation being given to the subject of the Masters of Business Administration program.[9] It has been found, for example, that the median salaries of graduates of the Harvard Business School plateau approximately fifteen years after the graduate enters business and, on the average, do not increase significantly thereafter. Thus, the growth of most business graduates seems to level off just at the time when men who are destined for top management typically show their greatest rate of advancement. This suggests that "men who get to the top in management have developed skills that are not taught in formal management education programs and may be difficult for highly educated men to learn on the job."

So disenchanted is Peter Drucker with management training that he has suggested that one of the qualifications for obtaining a management position be that the contender does *not* have a university degree.[10] Another writer says that "problem finding" is more important than problem solving and involves cognitive processes that are very different and much more complex. "While the analytical skills needed for problem solving are important, more crucial to managerial success are the perceptual skills needed to identify problems long before evidence of them can be found by even the most advanced management system. Since these perceptual skills are extremely difficult to develop in the classroom, they are now largely left to be developed on the job."[11]

C. G. Jung draws a distinction between two kinds of thinking: that which he calls "fantasy" thinking and that which he calls "directed" thinking. He says, "Directed thinking was not always as developed as it is today. The clearest expression of modern directed thinking is science and the techniques fostered by it. Both owe their existence simply and solely to energetic training in directed thinking."[12]

Although the development and insistence upon directed thinking may be modern, the identification of two types of thinking is most certainly not. Blaise Pascal devoted the first of his *Pensées* to the question of the difference between the mathematical and the intuitive mind. He said, "The reason that some intuitive minds are not mathematical is that they cannot at all turn their attention to the principles of mathematics. But the reason that mathematicians are not intuitive is that they do not see what is before them, and that, accustomed to the exact and plain principles of mathematics, and not reasoning until they have well inspected and arranged their principles, they are lost in matters of intuition where the principles do not permit such arrangement. They are scarcely seen; they are felt rather than seen; there is the greatest difficulty in making them felt by those who do not themselves perceive them." He continues, "There are then two kinds of intellect: the one able to penetrate acutely and deeply into the conclusions of given premises, and this is the precise mind; the other able to comprehend a great number of premises without confusing them, and this is the mathematical mind. The one has force and exactness, the other comprehension. Now the one quality can exist without the other, the mind can be strong and narrow and can also be comprehensive and weak."[13]

Perception ends in an idea; intellect in a logical formulation. Perception therefore concerns itself with a totality, with a whole, while the intellect concerns itself with parts. Perception concerns itself with the idea, the intellect with the fact that expresses that idea. Perception is immediate, timeless; intellect is in time, it passes through stages.

The marketing dimension is that dimension concerned with perceiving the idea that can be expressed by the company as the product. The commitment of the company is the sanction provided by the shareholder, employee, and market focused by the president through the medium of the idea of the company product. *The level of perception in an individual is therefore the counterpart of the marketing department within a company.*

The relation of perception to idea has already been dealt with at length in Chapter 16. It can be seen that there are different levels of ideas; some subsume others and, in turn, are subsumed by still others. A genius could be said to be a man who has the level of perception to perceive an idea that takes more than a lifetime to realize. Henry Ford perceived an idea, and that idea reverberates throughout the world. Picasso has structured the twentieth century for us. Each of us hears the world differently because of Beethoven, Bach, or the Beatles. Through his perception the original artist, thinker, or mystic opens a window onto the world; he gives the world a new idea, a new perspective.

Spengler points out "the history of a culture is the progressive actualization of the possibilities inherent in the idea, and fulfilment of these possibilities is its end."[14] Spengler returns repeatedly to the idea as the unifying element in history. Through the idea, he says, it is possible to "see each fact in the historical picture—each idea, art, war, personality, epoch—according to its symbolic content,

182 ZEN AND CREATIVE MANAGEMENT

and to regard history not as a mere sum of things without intrinsic order or inner necessity, but as an organism of rigorous structure and significant articulation, an organism that does not suddenly dissolve into a formless and ambiguous future when it reaches the accidental present of the observer."

Spengler saw the great problem for twentieth century as the careful exploration of the inner structure of the organic units through and in which world history fulfills itself; "to separate the morphologically necessary from the accidental, and, by seizing the *purport* of events, to ascertain the language in which they speak."[15] The industrial enterprise is one of the primary organic units through which and in which world history fulfills itself.

Thus we see that the first dimension of capacity is perception, and the level of idea that gives rise to work and the industrial enterprise is a function of the level of perception.

STRESS TOLERANCE

To do work it is first necessary to perceive the idea that reveals the dilemma. The higher the level of the dilemma, the longer the time span required to resolve it. Some ideas can be of such richness and of such power that it takes more than one lifetime for their implications to be expressed.

Hans Selye, responsible for initiating much of the research into stress, postulates that there is an energy that enables an organism to cope with stress. The energy is hypothetical as far as he is concerned, and he confesses that he does not know what this energy might be. "It is as though we have hidden resources of adaptability, or *adaptation energy,* in ourselves throughout the body. . . . Only when all our adaptability is used up will irreversible, general exhaustion and death set in . . . The term 'adaptation energy' has been coined for that which is consumed during continued adaptive work, to indicate that it is something different from the caloric energy received from food. . . .

We still have no precise concept of what this energy might be."[16]

Selye would no doubt agree that the realization of the idea is the ultimate aim of a man, and he sees each individual as different, having a different tolerance and a different level at which he can work. "In order to express yourself fully, you must first find your optimum stress level, and then use your adaptation energy at a rate and in a direction adjusted to the innate structure of your mind and body."[17]

Selye makes no distinction between psychological and physiological stress, and psychosomatic medicine generally agrees with this. If it is true that a consumable "something" underlies man's adaptation to stress, it would be true of psychological as well as physiological states. All disturbances of homeostasis, of what Selye calls "staying power," could be considered a source of stress. All activity leads to a "consumption" of adaptive energy.

Perceiving a problem means relating it to a structural as well as a temporal perspective. One must relate the problem to a structure by seeing what fits and what does not fit, what is integrated and what is not, whether it is a whole or whether parts are still unjoined. But the problem must also be seen from a historical perspective and in terms of what the future requires. Good decisions create the future out of the past and furthermore re-create the past in the face of the future. Churchill and Hitler were both conscious of history, and it was through this consciousness that much of their power was derived.

The manager must command both structure and time. "The manager cannot manage well unless he in some sense manages all. Specifically he must have some idea of what the whole relevant world is like, to be able to justify that which he manages, if managed correctly."[18]

The power to do work is based on this sense of "history." But these recognitions of fitness and of history bring with them the recognitions of incompleteness, of waste and risk, in fact of the dilemma itself. This gives rise to stress. This stress can be reduced either by surrendering the idea (failing), or by expressing the idea (succeeding). The situation becomes unbearable to the extent that the stress reaches and passes a given threshold. The level of this threshold is a function of what we shall call *stress tolerance*. The capacity to bear stress, to tolerate incompleteness, to carry the burden of waste and risk and to face and resolve the dilemma is stress tolerance. Managers must be those "who are comfortable in the presence of risk, who have a high tolerance for ambiguity and uncertainty."[19]

Stress is defined by Selye as a "state manifested by a specific syndrome which consists of all the non-specifically induced changes within a biological system . . . a triad of surprise, mastery and fatigue."[20] He underlines the importance of completion of all three phases of the stress-response cycle in all our activities as well as in all our passive sensations. To Selye, *this cycle is the biological basis of man's need to express himself and fulfill his mission.* "Man is constructed for this cycle. He should direct his life accordingly, neglecting no phase of it, and giving each manifestation of life the emphasis which fits his personal requirements."[21]

What Selye has to say about this cycle fits very well with what we have understood so far. The following quotation from Bertrand Russell's autobiography will perhaps help to show the way that stress is involved when realizing or expressing an idea. "The years from 1902–1910 were very painful to me. They were, it is true, extremely fruitful in the way of work, but the pleasure to be derived from the writing of *Principia Mathematica* was all crammed into the latter months of 1900 [surprise]. After that time the difficulty and labour were too great for any pleasure to be possible [mastery]. The last years were better than the earlier ones because they were more fruitful, but the only really vivid delight connected with the whole matter was that which I felt in handing over the manuscript to the Cambridge University Press."[22] Earlier Russell had described how the intellectual strain had been so great that he would often consider suicide as a way out, and felt that his intellect would never really recover from the strain imposed upon it by his labor (exhaustion).

The idea has been perceived, the dilemma held, the incompleteness realized, and the stress mounts. There is, one might say, a tension between the pole of "things as they are" and the pole of "things as they ought to be," and these two poles must be held in the process of completing work.

If one were to let go of "things as they are," one would soar off into space and the idea would degenerate into a shower of ashes. There would no longer be any vitality left in the situation at all. It could no longer generate time for its realization. Impatience, dogmatism, and boasts are the ways of the man for whom reality has lost its hold.

But all change must begin with a wish. If the idea is relinquished, if "what could be" is sacrificed for "what is" one has reneged, failed in his destiny. The idea dissipates, is destroyed, and the debris of experience causes rubble in the mind. It is meaningless and without spirit, and the vacuum created by the loss of the idea is filled by shame and remorse. World weariness, self-pity, and self-reproach are the lot of a man who has relinquished his idea. Growth stops and the whole point of life is lost.

We can therefore say that stress tolerance is related to organization. If perception is related to the marketing department, *stress tolerance has its counterpart in a company in the organization and manning department,* that is, the human resources or personnel departments of a company.

COMMUNICATION

The power to do work includes the power to perceive an idea, to hold that idea in the face of a dilemma, and to work out the implications of that dilemma. But it also includes sensitivity to the environment. This sensitivity implies an interaction between a system and its higher and lower systems, and could also be called empathy or even compassion. It manifests itself as communication. The level of communication is therefore considered to be the third dimension of capacity.

There are many people who can perceive an idea, who can hold onto the dilemma, but who are completely rigid and unflexible in their behavior. They can take all sorts of knocks, but nothing changes them—there is no growth as far as they are concerned. A growing man is one who is able to change both his idea and the dilemma in consequence of the experience that he receives from the world without abandoning either. This requires a capacity to respond to change.

This responsiveness is related to empathy, which in turn is the foundation of communication.[23] Without empathy there is interaction but not communication. The relationship of change, empathy, and communication was studied by an American psychotherapist, Carl Rogers, whose comments are worth noting. Change is not something, it is not an entity with specific attributes. In psychotherapy the clients who make progress do so by moving from a state of rigidity to one of flux. Rogers conjectured that there was a continuum through which clients pass in moving from rigidity to flux, and he discriminated seven stages in this continuum. This idea is important to our study because this continuum is that of the capacity for communication.

At first a person is out of touch with his own feelings. These feelings can be described as being remote or unowned. The sense of ownership, of being in control of and responsible for his feelings increases as the person moves along the seven stages of the process continuum. Accompanying this increasing awareness and communication with himself are several other shifts: a shift from incongruence to congruence; an awareness of problems and a willingness to solve them; and a change toward accepting meanings as tentative and the best possible rather than as absolute and true. As Rogers states, "The process involves a change in the manner in which and extent to which the individual is able and willing to communicate with himself in a receptive climate." It is as though a person unfreezes, starting off as a rigid block and becoming a bubbling and flowing stream.

"The process moves from a point of fixity where all the elements and threads described above are separately discernible and separately understandable, to the flowing peak moments of therapy in which all those threads become inseparably woven together. In the new experiencing with immediacy that occurs at such moments, feeling and cognition interpenetrate, self is subjectively present in the experience, volition is simply the subjective flowing of a harmonious balance of organismic direction. Thus, as the process reaches this point the person becomes a unity of flow, of motion. He has changed, but what seems most significant, he has become an integrated process of changingness."[24]

What Rogers describes as a continuum could also be looked upon as a scale of communication capacity: at the lower end is inhibited or closed communication; at the higher end would be openness to experience and receptivity to change. Rogers points out that "cases which by other criteria are known to be more successful, show greater movement on the process scale than less successful ones."[25] Also surprisingly enough, it has been found that successful cases begin at a higher level on the process scale than do unsuccessful ones. It would seem, therefore, that the process scale can be used as an assessment of people generally and that people differ in their "internal" and "external" mobility. What Rogers says, therefore, gives a further theoretical foundation for the idea that a third dimension to capacity exists, a dimension concerned with empathy.

Rogers' change or process continuum can be applied to an organization. Organizations could be plotted on this scale according to the degree of internal and external communication that exists within a company. A company would be low on the process continuum to the degree that it is fixed in its strategy, that is, the degree to which it serves only one of the dimensions within a company. A company that believes it is in business simply to make a profit would be low on Rogers' process continuum.

Within a company meaningful communication concerns decisions. Communications should be concerned either with decisions that have been made or with information required for decisions to be made. Indeed, an organization could be looked upon as a decision structure. This idea was developed when considering roles as territories and noting that the boundaries of roles are formed by decisions. A decision is to be distinguished from an opinion in that a decision has the means by which it can be made effective. To make a decision is an action. That which makes a decision effective within an organization is the command of the necessary financial and other resources. Budgets or, better still, resource feed flow systems are therefore the primary systems by which decision making, and therefore effective interaction or communication within an organization, is made possible. Finance could be considered to be the "carrier wave" of communication within a company.

Therefore the level of communication within a company is a function of the budget or resource feed flow system within that company. *Communication, in the sense described above for an individual, corresponds to the treasury and accounting functions within a company.*

Ability

In the same way that the three dimensions of capacity correspond to the three dimensions of organization as structure, so the abilities of a person correspond to the organization as process. Ability has three dimensions: skill, education, and compatability. In considering these three we shall see that skill corresponds to the product development dimension, education and experience to product processing, and compatibility to the sales/service dimension.

Skill is the first requirement necessary for expressing an idea. Skill may be mental or physical. In non-managerial work, motor skills are most necessary and there is a wide diversity, as well as level, of these skills. In managerial work, skills are mental and normally considered to be three in number. There are a number of tests designed to determine the level of skill of a person, and these normally are addressed to determining the level of ability to manipulate numbers, to comprehend verbal expressions or words, and to reason deductively and analogically.

Education and experience processes the product of skill into an organized whole, education being condensed and systematized experience. Skill enables a person to conceptualize and quantify plans, but experience provides the equipment and structures necessary to carry these plans into action. Without this equipment the plans are aborted.

Compatibility determines how much of that which has been developed by skill and processed through experience will be linked to the environment. People frequently fail to get a job simply because they do not fit in. There is an obvious level of compatibility concerned with religion, nationality, size, weight, sex, and other factors of people, even though the law prohibits discrimination on these factors. But compatibility has a more subtle aspect, and it is this subtle aspect that could legitimately be called an ability. Attention has been drawn to this fact by Edward Hall[26] who has pointed out that different cultures have different perceptions of time and space propriety. Compatibility requires that a person be sensitive to these requirements and capable of adjusting to them. Hall suggests that the United States may have failed to fit in through the failure of some Americans to be sensitive to the ways in which people of other countries handle space and time. He says, "Although the United States has spent billions of dollars on foreign aid policy, it has captured neither the affections nor the esteem of the rest of the world. In many countries today Americans are cordially disliked."[27] In the terms we are using it might be said that such Americans are low on the compatibility dimension.

The importance of ability to do work has been generally well recognized, and a rising level of sophistication in interviewing techniques can be seen, starting with the interviewer who simply decides whether or not the applicant will fit in. The more sophisticated interviewer also considers the experience of the applicant and a whole interviewing technique based on the application blank has been developed. Even greater sophistication is achieved through the application of mental and motor skill tests to the candidate. Ability is visible, and it is for this reason that it has been recognized. However, there are many who recognize that ability is not all, but, except for the work of Elliott Jaques, there has been no real attempt to explore capacity and find ways that it too, can be systematically taken into account.

The three capacity dimensions vary independently of each other. It is possible for a man to have very high perception, very low stress tolerance, and average empathy with others. Or alternatively, he might have a very low perception, very low stress tolerance, and high empathy with others. It could be said that the original thinker will have a high level of perception, that the generalist will have a high level of stress tolerance, and the good salesman will have a high level of empathy.

Not infrequently one finds people with considerable ability but relatively little capacity. One might find, for example, an engineer who can score high on tests, who has an adequate engineering degree, and who is able to fit in without difficulty, but who lacks both perception and stress tolerance and is low on communication. Alternatively, one might find people with great capacity and relatively little ability. This would set up considerable stress in an individual.

The situation of a man with small capacity and high ability is something like a company that has too much equipment or too many systems and must spend a disproportionate amount of time maintaining the systems and servicing the equipment. Alternatively, a man with too much capacity and too little ability is something like a company that has grown too fast: It has considerable potential in the market, its employees are well motivated, and it has very good credit facilities, but its systems are antiquated, its manufacturing systems and machinery are poor, and its ability to sell and service is lacking. Such a company would first need to set its house in order by establishing its process dimensions.

The company's systems, its standard practices and procedures, are similar to an individual's education. A company with a good set of systems that are well-indexed and easily accessible is like a well-educated man. On the other hand, a company with a poor set of systems is like an ill-educated man. A company with a good set of systems that are poorly indexed is something like a man who has an education but a poor memory and is, therefore, unable to make use of the education he has received. The skills that a company has could be related to the tools and machinery, equipment, and instruments that are available to the people.

Ability is the channel of expression for capacity. If this channel is too limited, too restricted, capacity cannot be expressed. We have already referred to the "idea" and

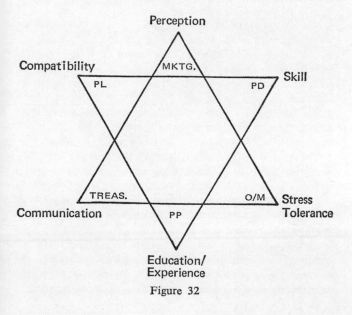

Figure 32

"fact," "structure" and "process," and now we have "capacity" and "ability." Broadly, capacity is the integrative aspect of a person and ability, the assertive aspect. We can now complete our paradigm and show the correspondence that might be said to exist between the structure of a company and the capacity of a person, and the process of a company and the ability of a person as in Figure 32.

18. ZEN AND THE BASIC POLARITY

Our study leads to a disturbing conclusion: *To be* at all, we must be in conflict, and from this conflict comes pain. Feelings of alienation do not come from something that the world either does to us or fails to do for us. Ordinary, everyday life threatens us with tedium and boredom on the one hand or stress and frustration on the other, and we look for something in the world to rescue us. All that we do as managers, consumers, and shareholders is a search for such a rescue. But this very search is the cause of the problem. Zen teachings would say that like a man who has turned his back on home, we search in vain for a place to rest.

For the Buddhist, the fact of suffering is basic: It is an axiom of Buddhism, the first noble truth, that everything suffers. Suffering comes from the basic polarity inherent in all things, and a molecule suffers no less than a man.[1] In man, however, there is a new characteristic: The polarity does not only inhere in the core of his being, but as we have seen, it is projected as what he calls his "life." This projection is made unconsciously and appears as a separation. It is this primary separation that sets up the ensuing dilemma—I am unique, but I am not the world and am therefore not complete; I am lacking in something that this world has. If I am to be whole, I must surrender my uniqueness, but will I not then lose my capability of reacting with others? Managers must come to terms with the basic polarity. Harry Levinson says, "The basic problem with which the executive has to contend is himself. The primary source of dilemmas which leaders face are their own inner conflicts. To lead successfully presupposes having much of one's own psychological house in order."[2]

Because managers have failed to put their psychological, indeed their spiritual house in order, the dilemmas mount. The more perceptive manager is aware that the business world is coming apart at the seams, not because there is anything inherently bad about that world, but because he himself is unable to cope with it. In the face of this and lacking an alternative, management development programs, emphasizing seminars and training, come into being. The logic is that if we are failing to cope, it is because there is something we are failing to do, and this is because there is something we yet have to know. But Zen practice will show that we do too much, we know too much.

Because we fail to weigh issues, to truly ponder the basis of our malaise, we are inclined to apply remedies to immediate and perceptible problems. In a company we set up a task force which on completion of its research issues a new practice. Alternatively, we find that another company has resolved a particular problem, and we import their solution to our own company. The effect of our seminars, task forces, and research is that we get piecemeal solutions that do not fit together. This generates new problems, more task forces, and more systems leading to more piecemeal approaches and more friction. It also leads to less and less meaning.

The meaning of something is derived from its relationship to a greater whole. Our analysis of company structure shows how this is true, shows how the meaning and contribution made by the shareholder has meaning only within the whole which includes the employee and market. The meaning of the product of a particular role likewise is to be found in the way that the product relates and interacts with other products.

The parts of a whole interact with each other—this may be a loose interaction, in which the whole has little or no structure, or it can be more pointed, in which case the interaction becomes communication, leading to higher levels of structure. But the structure makes its own demands and leads to communication becoming more pointed yet in competition. The "competitive spirit" derives from the need to communicate. The rugged individualist is simply trying to find his way into a wider world. We all strive to produce in order that what we produce can be accepted, applauded, or admired. Through our work we speak to the world in the hope that the world will speak to us, and we compete in reaction to the competitiveness of others and the demands of the structure.

But communication through competition is self-defeating. The eternal paradox is reaffirmed once more. Our life can be saved only by losing it; or conversely the effort to save our life causes us to lose that life. In our search for meaning we come full circle because we find once more that in order *to be* meaningfully—in order to live—we must be in conflict.

It would seem that an organization is to the mind what a telescope is to the lens of the eye; both the organization and telescope are subject to the laws governing their living counterparts. It is not surprising, therefore, that both organization and meaning have an ambiguous structure and process and they are alike in having a basic polarity inherent in them. Both organization and life dilemmas can be avoided through inauthenticity. Inauthenticity is its own kind of suffering; it is merely suffering avoided by suffering. Similarly, it is frequently the case that loss in creativity in the work situation is avoided through destroying creativity in work. How then can we deal with the dilemma in an authentic way? The poignancy of this question is even more pronounced when we recognize that authenticity calls for some pure act, an act that is unadulterated by ambiguity and contradiction, while as we know, a dilemma is the very source of contradiction and ambiguity. We seem to be ensnared and all our struggles serve only to bind the snare more tightly around us. We seem to be destined to destroy ourselves in our very effort to save ourselves. Is the seed of our own ultimate destruction really buried deep in the heart of each of us?

From one point of view the dilemma is cause for deep

despair. For example, Arthur Koestler writes, "the schizo-physiology inherent in man's nature and the resulting split in our minds, the old paranoid streak in man combined with his new powers of destruction, must sooner or later lead to geno-suicide."[3]

But, surprisingly, despair is not the only reaction that we might have. From the point of view of the Zen practitioner, the dilemma leads in quite the opposite direction, it leads to life and optimism:

> Magnificent! Magnificent!
> No one knows the final word.
> The ocean beds' aflame.
> Out of the void leap wooden lambs.[4]

Koestler's despair leads him to recommend a biochemical solution. He yearns for a pill that will restore "dynamic equilibrium" because he feels that we are in a way biological freaks that have lost their way. We are a mentally sick race, he says, and as such dead to persuasion. As nature has not provided the corrective remedy, we must provide it ourselves: "Nature has let us down, God seems to have left the receiver off the hook, and time is running out."[5] But if our understanding is right, then such a biochemical remedy would merely salvage man as a body at the expense of man as a whole—body/mind. We should destroy the holon to save the holon. If we destroy conflict to salvage meaning, our remedy itself may become the very disease. Koestler wants the biochemical pill to provide *dynamic* equilibrium; but it is the dynamism itself that is disturbing the equilibrium. Koestler sees so clearly the shadow and would rid us of it by turning out the light.

This is the problem and it has great relevance to industry. Without understanding it no viable organization is possible. Global wars are the final outcome of interpersonal conflict, the kind of conflict that we encounter daily, conflict that we in fact create through the pain that we inflict upon others. The territorial struggles of the super powers are simply magnified versions of interdepartmental conflicts. Each company has its own power politics; Machiavellian tactics were used by managers long before they became aware that their shifts and maneuvers had such ancestry. Let us not waste our time seeking who is tolling the bell—the rope is in our own hand. We must resolve our own schism before we can resolve the conflicts in the world. Unless we find a way to use conflict creatively, we shall have to abandon creativity altogether or perish.

Even at the most mundane level, this presence of conflict and our unwillingness and inability to deal with it creatively must be of concern to businessmen. Just as animals attack the trees in each other's territories rather than attack each other, so managers do not attack one another's person but overtly or covertly deliberately destroy each other's administrative systems. The amount of damage inflicted upon a company in this way is enormous, and as specialization and automation increase—while communication and participation decrease—this damage, and the attendant costs, will also increase. Even regarding the company simply from the perspective of the profit that it will generate, it is surely of great concern that so much profit is needlessly lost that might not have been lost were we able to deal with what we have called the basic polarity or the schizo-physiology of man.

Ours is not the first age to address this inner conflict and consequent pathological behavior. What is new is that ours is the first age in which there is no accepted way of handling these tensions and of giving them some kind of outlet. Every civilization of the past has recognized the inner polarity of people; each civilization has sought its own way for giving the conflict meaningful expression. This is one of the basic duties of religion. Moral and ethical codes have been based upon the recognition of the inherent destructive potentiality that each of us has and religious disciplines are designed to give us ways to reconcile the opposites that struggle within us. Myths and legends are often the stories of the way holy men and saints of the past have come to terms with themselves, stories of their "deaths" as restless, inert men and their "resurrection" as spiritually alive men.

Probably the most thorough-going approach to this schism is Buddhism, and one of the schools of Buddhism most suited to the West is Zen Buddhism. "Buddha" means "awakened"—awakened from the sleep, the restless inertia induced by the conflict of opposites. Because we are lazy our minds sink naturally to the lowest level of understanding, and we come to believe in the reality of opposition. Most of us believe the world is *really out there* with its own distinct and separate reality. Likewise we believe that we have a world "in here." We believe the mind is separate from the body, emotions are separate from thought, and good has a reality that is distinct from bad. We see nothing incongruent in searching for "everlasting peace," in asking where we go after death, or in searching to overcome once and for all suffering in the world. This fixation on the *reality of opposition* is our sickness, it is what a Zen Master called the "bumpkin sickness,"[6] and it can only be cured by our awakening. This is the simple, straightforward teaching of Zen—we must wake up. This does not mean that we gain some new insight, acquire some new knowledge or power. Insight, knowledge, and power are all downstream of opposition; awakening is upstream. Indeed Zen awakening is *awakening to the opposites as two valid ways of being*.

19. ZEN: CREATIVITY THROUGH THE DILEMMA

Zen is taught in Japan, but originated in India with the advent of the Awakening of an Indian prince named Gautama. From all accounts, the times of Gautama were very much like our own—restless, strife-torn, and at a spiritually low ebb. He was married, with one child, but in spite of all the luxury and ease to which he was subject as the son of a rich man, the need for a deeper meaning forced him to search for a new way. Through this search he came to a deep awakening and spent his remaining forty years of life teaching a simple but very profound way for attaining spiritual and mental health. This is called the Middle Way, as it eschews any extreme, and is a way open to all—men or women, monks or laymen, intellectuals or practical men, young or old. It is down-to-earth, emphasizing self-reliance and respect, hard work, common sense, and simplicity in all things. From India Buddhism traveled to China; from China it spread throughout Southeast Asia, through Korea, Vietnam, and Japan. Throughout the Far East Buddhism became remarkable as a way by which human beings are able to come fully into their own and to act and be in a complete, simple, and natural way. "A man of character is not expected to be led astray at all by other people. He is master of himself wherever he goes. As he stands all is right with him."[1]

The basis of Zen is Zazen. This is often mistranslated as "meditation," and it is very important to make the distinction between Zazen and meditation, not in any pejorative sense, but because there is a difference. The word "meditation" is derived from a Greek word *medonai* which means "to think about"; Zazen does not involve thinking about anything. *Za* in Japanese means "to sit," and "Zen" is a transliteration of the Chinese word *Ch'an,* which in its turn is the nearest that the Chinese can come to saying *Dhyana. Dhyana* is a Sanskrit word and can be approximately translated as "concentration," but a concentration of a particular kind and familiar to us as a consequence of our study of the dilemma. *The concentrated state of Zazen is a natural condition of the mind that arises from an unresolved dilemma.* In Zazen the automatic, habitual ways of coping with the dilemma are warded off. Of these ways, the one we use most persistently is surrendering to an automatic stream of consciousness. This dissipates concentration because basically *it is a steady stream of thought designed to use up energy that is generated naturally by the primordial dilemma.* This is the very opposite of Zazen. Thus, the concentration of Zazen differs from other forms of concentration in that an individual is not concentrating on *something,* and it is different from meditation in that conceptual thought is not used. The practitioner must awaken the mind without resting it on anything.

It is very hard work to awaken the mind in this way and it initially requires considerable effort—effort of a particular kind. This effort involves the sacrifice of all that would presume to offer itself as an alternative. At first these alternatives are quite obvious. Life problems and worries, projects and plans crowd the mind. The beginner is often confused and disheartened because the very application of his mind in this new way seems to stimulate the very thoughts and worries that he had hoped to quell. The struggle consists in allowing thoughts to well up without resting upon those thoughts, and this struggle is very great. But when the practitioner becomes adept, the stress and effort is transformed into tautness and the mind becomes ready, "like a drawn bow." As long as there is no reconciling idea, the mind is in a state of alert readiness. It is not a state of trance or dreaminess. Drowsiness does occur, but this is a condition that comes from falling away from the tautness. The "mind" is perceiving—in other words, it is fully active—but there is no content to the perceiving other than the act of perception itself. This act of perception is not a separate discrete act; it is the condition of wholeness and completeness that is the birthright of each of us.

Although Buddhism is a religion, it has no "beliefs"; there is no separate body of knowledge which the Buddhist must believe. Buddhism likewise does not deny, and it is not atheistic. Basic to Buddhism is this recognition of wholeness and completeness to which we have just referred. At first this may be known simply through an intellectual assent, but the awakening of Buddhism comes with the full cognition of this wholeness and completeness. The struggle in Zazen has always in the background, so to speak, the wholeness and completeness of the practitioner. In the middle ground is the dilemma which is experienced as a profound perplexity (in Zen it is known as the Great Doubt). In the foreground are the problems, worries, and confusions of everyday life. A Zen teacher seeks to arouse in the practitioner *wholeness and completeness and at the same time the dilemma.* The greater the teacher, the more he is able to do this. The great teacher uses all his skill to awaken and heighten the profound perplexity, the condition in which the mind is unable to settle on a comforting conclusion and equally unable to forage for a distracting thought. The teacher does this out of great compassion, knowing that it is only in the very center of the dilemma that creative perception is possible.

The two principal methods that the old Chinese and Japanese Zen masters used in their efforts to awaken and heighten the perception of the dilemma, to increase the experience of perplexity and doubt, were humiliation and the *koan.* Through humiliation the power of our compensations and illusions to shield us from the dilemma is broken. The *koan,* on the other hand, is a phrase or uttered statement that perfectly reflects the dilemma.[2]

The great value of Zen is that it enables us to use the *suffering* which is such a real and essential part of our life in a way in which it becomes integrated into our life as a whole. If he humiliates, the Zen Master is doing just what life is doing to us constantly, but he does it in a context in which we are able to grapple and come to terms with it. Without special training, humiliation and our confrontation by the enigmas of life must be side-stepped, avoided, suppressed, projected, or used in all the ways in which we use them only to find them flying back in our face like spittle on the wind. With special training, humiliation, coming ultimately from the powerlessness induced by our own inner contradictions, becomes a torch burning the dross that shrouds our original state, and with this purification comes increased clarity, strength, and humility.[3] No true creativity is possible without some prior destruction: As long as we rest on the security of our certainty, nothing new can come to us. But humiliation can only open us to ourselves, whether through the administrations of a teacher or the disinterested carelessness of a colleague or supervisor, provided we have the strength and courage to allow this opening to proceed. Zen training is therefore training for living creatively, training for the art of life. Through Zazen we may acquire the strength and courage to open ourselves to the world.

As we know, there are some questions which cannot be answered. For example, is Figure 15 a picture of a vase or of two faces? Yet there are some such questions that cannot be avoided.

The most famous of all *koans* is *Mu!* A monk once asked a Zen teacher whether even a dog has the same creative self nature as a man. It was a serious question and the monk wanted an answer. The teacher could have been stumped by the question because if he answered it either one way or the other he would be at fault. To say "yes" would cause him to fall into dualism, he would break the world into "have" and "have not," "dogs" and "men"; he would destroy in the monk's mind the inner togetherness, the very understanding of the whole that the monk is seeking when he asks his question and which the teacher is dedicated to awaken. If the teacher said "no," he would not be speaking the truth. If he walked away without answering, the monk would be left with his question. If he stayed and pointed out to the monk that the question could not be answered "yes" or "no," the monk's mind would be filled with thoughts of "if" and "but." What must the teacher do? This is the nature of a *koan,* and there are many such *koans*—reflections of dilemmas with which ego so generously but unwittingly confronts us. The teacher answered, *"Mu!"* which means "nothing" or "negation"—our nearest equivalent is the prefix "un."

Many generations of Zen practitioners have struggled with and awakened through the *koan "Mu!" Mu!* is used at first as a means to ward off the unwelcome stream of thought, later as a way of expressing the dilemma, then as a mirror of the mind itself as negation, as nothing, and beyond that it is found to be an expression of the awakened state itself. *Mu!* is the mind. It may seem quaint at first for a man to be concerned with "nothing," with negation. Earlier it was pointed out that men "have always resisted the idea that they are nowhere for no particular reason and that when events force them to contemplate the ultimate nowhere of their lives they go to pieces and act in ways which the majority of mankind would consider inhuman."[4] Considering this, it might seem to some now highly dangerous to contemplate "nothing."

However, it is neither quaint nor dangerous, but natural. We are naturally in a state of constant dialogue of "something and nothing," a dialogue of "form and emptiness." Territory is "somewhere" because it has boundaries; but on the other side of the boundaries is nothing. Territory and status both are a kind of dogmatic assertion within the dialogue, which, although not ending the dialogue, empty it of significance and meaning in the way that significance and meaning is possible for us.

It has always been said that man is unique because he has the capacity of contemplating his own death, because he has the capability of encountering the "tragic sense of life." But man is truly unique because he has the capability of entertaining the dialogue between something and nothing, and creativity is just that dialogue. But this capabil-

ity entails the capability to be at one with nothing, with
Mu! Through *Mu!* the spiritual spasm induced by the basic
polarity is eased and released. *Mu!* is something and nothing. *Mu!* is veritably the expression of our true nature.
The answer to the monk's question lay not with the dog, or
with the teacher, but with himself.

Because we project the basic dilemma we lose the freedom to be and not to be and crimp reality. Reality, be-
ingness, or itness, is paramount. We then *encounter* nothing in an alien way. It is rejected and so comes to us in
an unconscious, disorganized way that leads us to anxiety
and even horror—to that existential anxiety with its counterparts of loneliness, fear and death, and the malaise of
insecurity. In our rejection of nothing we are exiled to a
life of care. To regain freedom we must sacrifice "something," release our spastic grip and let go of the center of
the dynamic field we have buried under status and prestige
and defended through territorial claims and disputes. In
other words, we have to let go of what appears to give us
our psychological advantage. Territory relieves the inner
conflict by having a center and periphery. To have one is to
have both. The boundary gives us a place in the world,
and the center gives us security and therefore inner
strength. When the boundary is crossed we give up a place
in the world; when the center is gone our strength is
sapped. Humiliation and loss of status and territory are the
same event. By our resistance to humiliation we entrench
ourselves in the center and seal ourselves off from the very
interchange that gives us meaning. We seal our boundaries
and prevent anything new from arising. Furthermore, by
resisting humiliation, we resist coming down to earth and
are forced to climb forever the illusory ladder of success
and status.

This sacrifice of "something" is a struggle. A struggle
that leads to a state of concentrated awareness. In this state
of concentrated awareness the practitioner has resolved the
problem of the dilemma and conflict by its total expression. In Zazen we are ourselves naturally: not conquering
the world, nor oppressed by the world, but one with the

world. The world is through us. Zazen is so natural that one can only marvel at the depth of our plight that we can come to consider it as unnatural.

Zazen can satisfy our highest aspirations—we are one with the creative power of the universe. We can know this directly and can build around this, knowing a life that is inspired and fulfilled by that knowing. Zazen is not a way to become superman, produce extrasensory capabilities, or get one up on others. There is no end to our perfectability, and the scope for growth is unlimited. This does not, however, mean that it is of value only to those who have a profound spiritual aspiration. Just as there is no end to growth or enlightenment, so, strictly speaking, is there no beginning to Zazen, no beginning to practice. Anyone who has seriously thought through a problem has engaged in Zazen to some extent when, having pushed his thinking to its limits, he nevertheless tries to go further to penetrate the problem. Moments of intense grief, anxiety, and pain can lead us to suspend ideas and remain in a condition of unresolved dilemma. There is a wonderful story of a lady from Michigan[5] who in her student days was so perplexed by the meaning of life that she came to struggle with this perplexity day and night until she entered fully this state of unresolved dilemma. She even went so far as to break through into an awakening, which was later confirmed as valid by Zen Master Yasutani Roshi who visited America periodically and taught Zen there. This awakening is the highest aspiration of human beings, and through Zen it is attainable by any one of us.

20. ZEN AS A DISCIPLINE FOR MANAGERS

Zen can be practiced anywhere anytime. No special conditions are necessary. Indeed it is said that Zen practiced in the heat and fury of everyday life is a thousand times more valuable than Zazen practiced in the quiet of a Zazen hall. "For penetrating to the depths of one's own true nature, and for attaining vitality valid on all occasions, nothing can surpass the practice of Zen in the midst of activity. . . . The power or wisdom obtained by practicing Zen in the world of action is like a rose that rises from the fire: it can never be destroyed. The rose that rises from the midst of flames becomes all the more beautiful and fragrant the nearer the fire rages."[1] However, most of us require long training before we can practice Zazen freely in everyday life. It is normal for most of us to have to take up a definite posture, give attention to our breathing, settle the focus of our mind, and usually this requires some sort of schedule.

Zazen means "sitting" Zen and this sitting posture is the way that one can practice Zen initially. It is best to have the posture demonstrated by a teacher and to have one's posture corrected by him. In Zazen the practitioner sits with legs crossed in the traditional Buddha posture, with the hands held in one of several ways. If it is too difficult or painful to sit in the full posture, variations are possible, including the variation of sitting upon a chair. Anyone who seriously practices Zazen, however, learns that undoubtedly the full position of sitting with each foot resting on the opposite thigh is the preferable posture.

Whatever posture is adopted, it is most important to give attention to certain essentials. The spine must be kept straight and the posture should be grounded in a natural "center of gravity." One should not be rigid in the fashion of a military guard, but should sit in the fashion of a strong, sturdy tree well-rooted in the earth out of which it grows naturally.

Body-mind is a holon—mind and body are not two parallel states nor can they be reduced one from the other. In being a holon a sturdy posture is the counterpart to a taut mind. When the beginner tries to bring the mind to rest through the effort to awaken it without resting it upon anything he invariably tries in a mistaken way to suppress thoughts. This effort to quiet the mind through repressing thought is reflected in a tense body state, the spine normally crouches forward, the shoulders become hunched, and the breathing becomes shallow and irregular and jerky. To help the beginner, therefore, certain emphasis is given to different aspects—to the way the hands are held, to the breathing, and so on—but of all the emphases, none is perhaps so important as the straight, erect spine.

If one is to sit in an erect posture, then the center of gravity of the posture must be low. Most of us in the West have a center of gravity in the head, whereas in the East the center of gravity is located more frequently in the lower belly or *hara*. This explains the rather awkward-looking posture of the Oriental when posing for a photograph. In the West we hold the head up, while the Oriental seems to push out the belly. Head up, chest out, stomach in! is the way of the West. This emphasis on "head up" brings attention up into the back of the neck and shoulders, and we become stiff-necked and proud. To "hold one's head high" is associated with a feeling of pride. It is as though we were trying to elevate ourselves off the earth. The *hara* region is that region below the level of the navel. When we sit erect we feel the energies and attention naturally settling into this lower area of the body. If we sigh deeply, we can feel a sense of relaxing of the upper chest and shoulder areas and a natural gathering together at the lower levels of the trunk. Furthermore, there is a specific point, about two inches below the navel, at which the energies seem to gather in the most concentrated form. If one brings the attention to rest naturally at this point, it gives the whole body-mind a wonderful sense of poise and well being. Anyone who practices the martial arts will be very familiar with this point. Indeed, unless they are, they cannot practice judo, aikido, karate, or kung fu.[2] The vital energies of the body follow the attention, and when the attention is held naturally at rest at this point, called the *tanden,* the energies well up but remain in reserve and one acquires a responsiveness while remaining completely relaxed. There is a marvelous beauty in the judo champion's movements. He seems almost gangling as he walks toward his opponent. He seems so relaxed as to be almost sleepy, but in a flash he crouches, leaps, and finishes his movement. When the attention is in the head the energies also well up, but it is almost impossible to remain relaxed—tension and restlessness, useless jerky thinking, anger and irritability all come from the arousing of energy and the need to dissipate it. Yet this energy is the very same energy with which we can contain stress and with which we are creative. Thus, locating the energies and attention in *hara* is not only of value to the martial artist but is also of equal value to the businessman, who no less needs to be as responsive and incisive and who no less needs to use wisely his vital forces.

However, most people find it is difficult at first to collect the attention at the *hara.* The mind constantly rises up straining at the diaphragm, tightening the chest, cramping the throat, and bringing the brows together in a deep furrow. Therefore, as a further aid, Zen Masters have taught practitioners to bring the hands together in a distinct posture. The right hand is held with the palm up, the fingers straight along the front of the lower belly. The left hand is held likewise and laid on top of the right. The thumbs are brought together in such a way that they are not quite touching yet not quite separate. The thumbs with the fingers make an oval, and the whole posture is taut but not rigid. A perceptive teacher will know the condition of the practitioner's mind simply by observing the condition of the hands. It is interesting to note that control of the thumbs takes up a great deal of the brain area, an area that is out of proportion to the size of the thumbs themselves. It is also probable that much of the peace and satisfaction that comes from handicrafts—particularly those such as knitting, rug hooking, and crocheting—comes from the thumbs being at peace in activity. Holding the hands in this posture soothes and cools the entire system in a natural way.

The beginner is also encouraged to regulate his breathing, but again this regulation is done naturally and simply. The practitioner is told to count the breaths, counting one for the first inhalation, two for the following exhalation, three for the next inhalation, and so on, up to ten. The teacher will emphasize that the breath itself should not be interfered with, no effort should be made to breathe deeply or shallowly, softly or loudly, with the chest or with the belly. The practitioner would simply be told that he should follow the breath while counting up to ten. The teacher will vary the instruction by having the practitioner count only the exhalations, or only the inhalations.

This counting and following the breath enables the practitioner to gain an awareness of the profound relation that there is between breathing and the mind. The word "spirit" comes from the Latin word for breath: *spiritus*. Following and counting the breath enables one to gain profound intuitive awareness of the meaning of this relation. Through following the breath one can see clearly into the meaning of the holon and appreciate for oneself the profound intuition that is summed up in Zen by the phrase "Not two, not one" that we have used as a basis in our explanation of the structure/process of an organization and in other places. This intuition comes as a by-product of a simple, straight-forward process. It is of great importance that a practitioner does not dwell on this sort of thing but remains dedicated to following and counting the breaths. But it is nevertheless true to say that just in this new awareness alone the racking dichotomies of either/or come to rest to some degree within us.

By bringing our awareness to bear on breathing in this way, without interfering or attempting to control our breathing in any way, we find that it naturally becomes finer and deeper. We naturally breathe readily from the diaphragm and use the upper chest muscles much less. The cardio-vascular system is stimulated and relaxed, blood pressure drops, and the autonomic nervous system is revitalized. Many practitioners find that they spontaneously break out in a sweat, not from effort but from relaxation. Many weep from sheer relief and others are unable to control guffaws of laughter, not from thought but as a spontaneous reaction of the body-mind to this entry into a way that tones up the whole system.

In Zen temples a further aid is used to deepen Zazen. Monitors, chosen from among the most advanced practitioners, strike practitioners on the shoulders with a specially designed piece of wood. In Japanese it is called a *kyosaku*, while in America it is simply called a paddle. It is shaped like a paddle, about three feet in length and three inches wide and one-half inch thick at the end that strikes the shoulder. The monitor is carefully trained to strike in such a way that the paddle does not hit the bone and a good monitor, even though he may strike quite hard, does not bruise the muscles of the shoulder at all. At first sight, this practice of striking the practitioners is rather surprising, particularly to those who believe that a way such as Zen leads people to be dreamy or withdrawn, and who believe that Zen is a way for people to escape the pain and difficulties of life. But for someone who is practicing deep Zazen the paddle can be a source of great stimulation. A monitor does not use the *kyosaku* in any punitive sense at all; it is in no way an instrument of admonishment, and a Zen Master would carefully select monitors who would not fall into the error of using the *kyosaku* without compassion and full regard for the practitioner. In a good temple monitors would only come from among those who had awakened to the truth.

To help deepen their practice and to heighten the possibility of awakening, Zen practitioners gather together in groups, sometimes up to fifty or more, for a week's Zazen. During such a retreat—*sesshin*—the practitioner devotes his entire energies to Zazen. Many will practice with but a few hours' sleep a night and continue through the day and night in a state of unswerving concentrated awareness. Such *sesshins* are invigorating in a way difficult to describe. However, except for the more advanced practitioner, they would be difficult indeed to tolerate without there being monitors skilled in the use of the *kyosaku*.

Zen Master Yasutani said that there were five forms of Zen.[3] He said that outwardly these five forms of Zen appear to be the same, and common to them all is an erect sitting posture, correct breathing, and concentration or unification of the mind. But there are also basic and important differences between these five ways. Yasutani's purpose in distinguishing these five forms was to enable his students to define their goal more clearly. The first of these he called "Ordinary Zen," and this form, free from any philosophical or religious content, is for anybody and everybody. Through the practice of ordinary Zen a manager could learn to control his mind and mobilize his energy in a way that he could never imagine to be possible. This mobilization of energy would make way for a more persistent yet dynamic approach to work, for greater flexibility, and for a deep awareness of our place in the scheme of things which comes from liberation.

Yasutani points out that it never occurs to most of us to try to control the mind, and it is an aspect of basic training that is missed entirely by our education. Yet with a mind filled with random thoughts, incapable of being directed for any length of time, we learn with great difficulty. Moreover, what we learn is difficult to retain because we have learned improperly. "Indeed, we are virtually crippled unless we know how to restrain our thoughts and concentrate our minds. Furthermore by practicing this very excellent mode of mind training, you will find yourself increasingly able to resist temptations to which you have previously succumbed and to sever attachments which had long held you in bondage. An enrichment of personality and a strengthening of character inevitably follow since the three basic elements of the mind—intellect, feeling, and will—develop more harmoniously."[4] He says that this form of Zazen is more beneficial for the cultivation of the mind than the reading of countless books on ethics and philosophy.

Zazen, therefore, offers an antidote to the pressure of the dilemma and to executive stress. Instead of introjecting the dilemma in a dwindling spiral of anxiety, withdrawal, and further anxiety, and instead of projecting it in a vicious circle of hostility and mutual struggle, we can, to an increasing degree, incorporate this dilemma in a world that is neither subjective nor objective, a world in which work is the natural expression of the dilemma as the exercise of discretion within limits. Work balanced by Zazen can provide a natural way to deal with our schizophysiology.

Work plays an important part in Zen. During *sesshin* practitioners do not sit constantly. Some of the time is devoted to chanting, to exercise, to attending to the teacher as he gives his understanding of Zen. Some of the time is also given to work. Man was made for work:

"Hyakujo, the Chinese Zen master, used to labor with his pupils even at the age of 80, trimming the gardens, cleaning the grounds and pruning the trees. The pupils felt sorry to see the old teacher working so hard, but they knew he would not listen to their advice to stop, so they hid his tools.

"That day the Master did not eat. The next day he did not eat, nor the next. 'He may be angry because we have hidden his tools,' the pupils surmised. 'We had better put them back.'

"The day they did the teacher worked and ate the same as before. In the evening he instructed them: 'No work, no food.'"[5]

Putting out work and receiving back food are not two separate activities. A man is his world, and it is through work that he discovers this world. Each of us must work for ourselves, but we can only do this if we work for others. This is evident to anyone who gains satisfaction from his work. I can only get back what I put out, or putting this the other way round, there is a cost for everything. There is an exquisite justice in the world which is nowhere brought out so clearly as in work. In working I give myself to the world, and in eating I receive the world into myself. Working and eating are not two, not one. Work when it is done well is a form of Zazen. Work which is done during a *sesshin* trains the practitioner to realize this fully. This points up that Zazen is not something simply to practice at specific times of the day and in specific and specialized circumstances. Much of the work that is carried out in a Zen temple is physical work, and it is important to realize that managerial work can also be a form of Zazen.

Ours is a fast changing world. Not only are there more changes occurring, but the rate of change is accelerating. We are constantly called upon to adjust to changes, and the threat that managers face more than any other is the threat of obsolescence. Overnight they may find that the skill and experience they have acquired through years of training and work no longer fit the needs of the time. They find that they must change or perish. Yet to change at all, even to change our minds, means that we must open ourselves. This opening is the great challenge. To do so means that we must face humiliation. To fail to do so means that we must cling more desperately to our status and territory. Territory is a step toward mind, but by sinking back to territory we regress along the evolutionary path, we retreat to inertia. To stay alive we must go forward. To do so we must change and this requires courage. Zazen is a way to acquire the courage to change and the discipline of Zen is therefore a discipline for adaptability.

Our industrial society is guilty of incredible pollution and plunder which extends beyond simply fouling the rivers and air or wasting energy and other non-renewable resources. A company feeds on ideas. Among its waste products must be included the husks that once contained the fruit long since gone. Obsolete managers who are no longer creative and therefore adaptable to change block up the productive process and cause it, in turn, to become antiquated and resistant to change. The problem that industry must face is that as change increases in pace, so the proportion of those who have failed to adapt must increase also, and the age at which such failure occurs must grow younger. Is industry to be guilty of people pollution as well? Would industry simply dump those who cannot adjust?

There are two solutions that are preferred: either premature retirement or "retraining." Premature retirement simply transfers the problem from industry to society at large and seems as unsatisfactory an answer as pouring waste products into the rivers, lakes, and oceans. "Retraining" comes from the same mentality as recycling old bottles and might work if people were merely old bottles. Retraining will simply increase the stress on the system of those being retrained. It increases the need to change without increasing the capacity to change, and *it is the capacity to change that will solve the problem of obsolescence.* Education at best enables a person to express what he perceives, and at worst it destroys his ability to perceive at all. Resistance to change is a withdrawal by reaffirming what is, that is, by clinging to whatever has already been perceived and expressed. It is this that prompts the cynic to say that few men think, most simply rearrange their prejudices.

The highest aim of Zazen is liberation. This means to *free us so that we can live fully in accordance with the nature of things, fully in accordance with change.* A primary perception that ensues from Zazen is the no-thingness of things. "The self nature of each existence is change itself . . . Every existence is a momentary form appearing according to prevailing conditions, without a fixed form of its own."[6] This is known as the doctrine of emptiness. Emptiness means that there is constant change. What we

call "things" are simply different gradients of change.
Nothing endures, but some changes are more slow than
others. In recent years we have come to discover this truth
for ourselves in the West.

That Zazen frees us to live in accordance with change is
shown most vividly, most dramatically in the manner in
which the true man of Zen faces death—the greatest
change of all. Zen literature sparkles with the gems of
hundreds, perhaps thousands of poems and stories written
at the time of a Zen Master's death or about his manner of
dying:

> Riding this wooden upside-down horse,
> I'm about to gallop through the void.
> Would you seek to trace me?
> Ha! Try catching the tempest in a net.

> For seventy-two years
> I've kept the ox well under.
> Today, the plum in bloom again,
> I let him wander in the snow.[7]

"Almost blind at the age of ninety-six and no longer
able to teach or work about the monastery, Zen Master
Yamamoto decided it was time to die, so he stopped eating. When asked by his monks why he refused his food, he
replied that he had outlived his usefulness and was only a
bother to everybody. They told him, 'If you die now
[January] when it is so cold, everybody will be uncomfortable at your funeral and you will be an even
greater nuisance, so please eat!' He thereupon resumed eating, but when it became warm again he stopped, and not
long after quietly toppled over and died."[8]

"Just before he passed away, at the age of sixty, Bassui
sat up in the lotus posture and to those gathered around
him said, 'Don't be misled! Look directly! What is this?'
He repeated it loudly, then calmly died."[9]

We cannot sit in Zazen even for a short while without a profound change coming to us in our understanding of change, because Zazen is the discipline of change, and the degree to which a person can cope with change and the unexpected is the measure of the depth of his Zazen and of his enlightenment. We have to be able to change if we are to fully realize our potential and take up the birthright that is naturally ours, and when we thwart this drive to be what we are we end in neurosis. Noögenic neuroses are those that arise through the frustrations of the spirit. Instead of natural freedom we become bound by our prejudice backed by terror.

The freedom of Zazen is not the freedom to behave arbitrarily. The free man may behave in an unexpected, even outrageous way; but freedom does not come from capriciousness, nor by practicing outrageous acts. The truly free man acts in such a way that the full potential of each moment is realized through him. It is from the respect that he has of the limitations and potentialities of the situation that the Zen practitioner respects the profound truth of karma.

Karma is the spiritual counterpart of the Newtonian axiom that for every action there is an equal and opposite reaction. The doctrine of karma is based upon the understanding that change is the rule and that fixity is but an appearance. However, this change is not arbitrary but according to a pattern or structure.

According to the understanding that is acquired through awakening, all fixed forms (including that which seems to be the most fixed of all—the form "I") are shown to be but an accumulation or center of forces which themselves are coming into being or passing away. In a company, for example, there is no fixed form. There is no such thing as "a company." To say that the company does this or that— "the company has been good to me" or "the company has expanded"—is but a convenient way of saying the nexus of forces issuing along many dimensions expresses itself in this or that way.

Possibly the nearest that the West has come to understanding karma is in music. A piece of music could be looked upon as the karma of a musical idea: At any given time the composer is at liberty to introduce any tone that he likes, but his choice will be tempered by the total musical expression—all that has gone before, all that is to come. A "good" piece of music is a whole, a unity, in which the full potential of that unity has been expressed. The musician, therefore, does what is right. He selects what is fit. The great work of art is simple, it is right, it obeys the laws of its own structure, it fulfills its own karma.

> For the truly enlightened man
> Subjection to the law of cause and effect
> And freedom from it are but one truth.[10]

Karma is often translated as the law of cause and effect, but this is inadequate. This inadequacy occurs because the translator has to fall back upon the Weltanschauung of his own culture. We can see now that karma is none other than structure/process in action. Our understanding of an organization provides the basis for the true understanding of karma. A company is a microcosm of the universe. It is a cosmos, a self-perpetuating system. If we carefully understand the interaction of commitment, process, and structure, we shall have a way to free ourselves finally from the restraints imposed upon us by a philosophy that causes us to choose between two mutually exclusive alternatives: the alternatives of free will and determinism.

In the same way that the role of the president of a company has been distorted by an organizational fixation on profits, so our lives have become distorted by an artificial preference for material reality. This fixation causes a split to occur—the management/employee split—and dualistic logic must prevail. In such a situation products cannot emerge from an organic unified whole, but goals must be imposed through a power hierarchy. We also find that we must discipline ourselves to operate in such an unnatural environment. We have to exercise self-control and the true expression of potential is impossible. We sit aching under the weight of brute, unresolvable dilemmas. In desperation we take sides, shed parts of our experience, and cling to territory and status in self-defense. Instead of living in a beautiful, changing, and free-flowing world of hierarchic ideas that come to maturity and then change into new ideas, we cling stubbornly to facts. Those who are able grab the control of resources, fend off the others, and turn them into dependent or hostile "staff" personnel. In our personalities we find complexes that break away and then return to haunt us. Instead of work being the challenge of turning limitation into resources through recognizing it as the exercise of discretion within limits, work becomes the brute application of power in constricted but crumbling circumstances.

The full depths of karma are ineffable, but our understanding of the framework of organization and the analysis that we have made of work is a tentative expression of some of these depths. Karma is liberation within the total structure of what is. This total structure is constantly seeking expression and finds this expression according to the degree of enlightenment of the consciousness through which it is being expressed. We are entirely free to commit ourselves within the structure of our experience and this commitment will be realized in behavior, that is, in our process. This process creates products—seeds—which in their turn give rise to structures, limitations on our commitment, and subsequent behavior. "All that we are is the result of our ideas and their expression: it is founded on these ideas, it is made up of them." This is the Buddhist teaching in the *Dhamappada*.

This same idea is expressed by Herbert Guenther, a Western writer on Buddhism, in his attempt to explain karma. A quotation is given from his book and a few words added in brackets so that the reader may tie in more closely what he says with what we have said so far:

> In a causal situation that cause is not an external agent acting upon something inert, but is this situation itself [structure], and the control or directive operation [process] is intrinsic to the situation as a whole. This implies that the effect [product] also is not something extraneous, but is an emergent arising within the process as such. Although such an emergent implies a "forward reference" [objective], it would again be wrong to describe the process as a "pursuit of an end" [management by objectives].[11]

Zen Buddhism is a legitimate concern for managers. The ideas of Buddhism help in understanding the structures in which we have to work, and Zazen gives the discipline to act in accordance with these structures. Through Zen Buddhism we may be liberated as managers and people so that we are capable of doing precisely what is necessary. In this way, each moment is a creative moment and each act is an act of creation.

APPENDICES

APPENDIX I

Example of a Decision Table

SUBJECT OF DECISION	PRESIDENT	R/D	SALES SERVICE	FINANCE	MARKETING
NEW AND EXISTING PRODUCTS	1. Decide priority price and extent of service to be given to new products.	1. Decide whether there are any servicing difficulties that would preclude the company from taking the new product.	1. Decide lead time required to prepare for release of new products.	1. Decide economic guidelines to be used for pricing new products for sale and rental or lease.	1. Decide methods of keeping in contact with new product developments.
		2. Decide appropriate method and equipment to use for servicing products.	2. Decide training required by sales personnel to sell new products.	2. Decide amortization period for products being leased or rented.	2. Decide which new products should be investigated.
		3. Decide what training is required to service products.	3. Decide quantity, location and method of storing items in local warehouses.		3. Decide which new products should be tried out by company.
		4. Decide amount of time to be given to training and personnel to give the service training.	4. Decide who should install new products.		4. Decide timing of introducing new products into company.
		5. Decide lead time required by R/D department for new products.	5. Decide method of ensuring that product is installed to customers' satisfaction.		5. Decide amount and type of advertising to be used for launching new product.

6. Decide price to pay, method of ordering, supplier and quantity of new and existing products to be purchased.

7. Decide price at which new and existing product will be sold, rented or leased.

8. Decide specific selling points of products.

9. Decide minimum and maximum product inventory levels.

6. Decide amount of time between sale and delivery of appliance to customer.

7. Decide best method of disseminating information about technical servicing of products.

8. Decide amount of servicing that will be given to appliances.

9. Decide type availability and quantity of materials, tools, and appliance parts to be carried.

10. Decide who will service appliances.

11. Decide method of obtaining information from customer about service required.

12. Decide who will receive and relay customer information.

6. Decide minimum inspection to be given to new and existing products.

7. Decide installation specifications for new and existing products.

8. Decide materials to be used for installing and repairing new and existing products.

9. Decide minimum maintenance requirements for new and existing products.

10. Specify minimum skills required to carry out servicing and set written tests to ensure that these skills exist.

11. Decide method of discovering problems being experienced in the field and of resolving those problems.

APPENDIX II

Dilemmas Involved in Setting Up a Salary Administration System

TOTAL SYSTEM

The system must be economic in terms of costs for implementation and administration.

The system must be pragmatic in that it ensures WCP in equilibrium as far as possible.

The system must be complete and cover the full range of work and all necessary roles.

The system must be capable of being understood and accepted by the employees and those using it.

In practice this dilemma is expressed as:

1. Take up as little time as possible in training analysts and evaluation group, in writing the descriptions and analyses and in evaluating the roles (where 500 - 1,000 roles are in question the time can be considerable).

Set up as many grades as possible so that each difference in level of work is compensated by an appropriate salary.

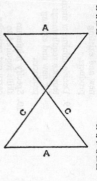

2. Ensure that analysts are trained to get all information and that evaluation team understands all the facts about the roles that they are called upon to evaluate.

Set up as few "boundaries" as possible recognizing that the more boundaries there are the greater the likelihood is that there will be boundary skirmishing.

DILEMMAS IN WRITING THE POLICY

DILEMMAS OF JOB DESCRIPTION

1. Job Description should be as simple as possible each statement being succinct and independent of other statements. (It should follow a basic convention in order that differences in description format alone should not imply a difference in content or level, descriptions should involve as little work as possible.)

Description must enable role to be evaluated, i.e. compared to others.

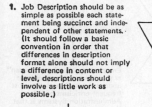

2. Job description and analysis must contain as much detail as necessary in order to capture the spirit as well as the content of the role as well as to satisfy the incumbent that sufficient is known of his role to enable an adequate evaluation to be made.

Method of description must relate to descriptions of roles undertaken for Organizational Analysis and Role Specifications.

DILEMMAS OF JOB EVALUATION

Use as straightforward and simple an evaluation system and factors as possible to cut down costs in training, explaining and administering.

Involve as few people in the evaluation process as possible in order to simplify the program. If there are too many involved, it becomes difficult to schedule meetings and to maintain a consistency of judgment as well as there being a greater likelihood of group pressure building up.

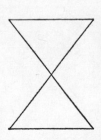

Use as sophisticated an evaluation procedure as necessary in order to take into account role differences.

Involve as many people in the evaluation process as necessary in order to gain acceptance of the system. Each group in the company should feel that it is represented in the group.

DILEMMAS IN WRITING THE POLICY

Set up as simple a policy as possible with as few exceptions and special considerations as possible. Alter as infrequently as possible, each alteration calling for more training, further adjustment and increased likelihood for misunderstanding.

Ensure policy takes into account local problems and local differences. Establish differential grade where possible.

Put in as much detail as necessary and word as tightly as necessary to avoid ambiguity and points being overlooked. Loose wording leads to a steady erosion of policy and allows "gray" areas to develop.

Ensure that policy is as "human" as possible to allow people to understand it. One of the most frequent criticisms of Salary Administration Systems is that they are too esoteric.

NOTES

Opening Quotations

1. Keynes, Maynard, *Religion and the Rise of Capitalism,* quoted by R. H. Tawney (208) (New York: Mento 235, 1954).
2. Fromm, Erich, *The Revolution of Hope* (New York: Harper & Row, 1968).

Foreword

1. Maruta, Dr. Yoshio, Chairman, Kao Corp., reported by D. W. Jackson, Half Lotus Inc. (*Intersect,* June 1991).
2. Kobayashi, Shigeru, President, SONY, *Creative Management* (American Magazine Association, New York, 1966).
3. Heidegger, Martin, *Discourse on Thinking* (New York: Harper Torch Books, 1966), p. 56.
4. Koestler, Arthur, *The Ghost in the Machine* (London: Pan Books, 1967), pp. 194–98.
5. Schumacher, E. F., *Small Is Beautiful, A Study of Economics as Though People Mattered* (New York: Harper & Row, 1973), p. 50. "From an economist's point of view, the marvel of the Buddhist's way of life is the utter rationality of its pattern— amazingly small means leading to extraordinarily satisfactory results. . . . Buddhist economics is the systematic study of how to attain given ends with the minimum means."

Chapter 1

1. Bennett, J. G., *The Dramatic Universe,* Vols. I–IV (London: Hodder & Stoughton, 1956, 1961, 1966, 1967). Bennett has developed a study of systematics. It is this study that provides much of the theoretical underpinning of the ideas explored in this book. The definition of a system is taken from his work.
2. Bernal, J. D., *The Origin of Life* (London: Weidenfeld & Nicholson, 1969). "Life is a partial, continuous, progres-

sive multiform and conditionally interactive self-realization of the potentialities of atomic electronic states."

3. Bennett, J. G., *The Dramatic Universe*, Vol. I, explores the notion of Being as "inner-togetherness."

4. ———, *The Dramatic Universe*, Vol. II, explores the importance of the triad as a manifestation of will.

5. Brown, Wilfred, *Explorations in Management* (London: Heinemann, 1960), p. 244.

Chapter 2

1. Lewin, Kurt, *Field Theory in Social Science*, ed. Dorwin Cartwright (New York: Harper Torch Books, 1951), p. 11. "Using the construction of a 'system in tension' for representing psychological needs definitely presupposes a field theory. Conceptually, tension refers to the state of one system relative to the state of surrounding systems. The essence and the purpose of this construct is to include a tendency for change in the direction of equalization of the state of neighboring systems."

2. Koestler, Arthur, *The Ghost in the Machine* (London: Pan Books, 1967), p. 65.

Chapter 3

1. Galbraith, J. K., *The New Industrial State* (Boston: Houghton Mifflin, 1967), p. 84.

2. Fausch, David A., *Business Week*, September 25, 1971. See also Mace Myles, *Directors: Myth & Reality* (Boston: Harvard Business School Division of Research).

3. Ibid.

4. Ibid.

5. Dale, Ernest, *Organization* (New York: American Management Association, Inc., 1970).

6. Drucker, Peter, *The Age of Discontinuity* (New York: Harper & Row, 1968), p. 205.

7. Galbraith, J. K., op. cit., p. 59.

8. Ibid., p. 110.

9. Drucker, Peter, op. cit., p. 189.

10. Galbraith, J. K., op. cit.

Chapter 4

1. Chang, Garma C. C., *The Buddhist Teaching of Totality* (University Park, Pa.: Pennsylvania State University Press, 1971), p. 11. "This system of higher realms embracing lower ones is envisioned in a structure consisting of 'layers' extending ad infinitum in both directions . . . This is called in the Hwa Yen vocabulary *realms-embracing-realms*."

2. Levitt, Theodore, "Marketing Myopia," *Harvard Business Review*, July–August 1960, pp. 275–76.
3. Ibid.
4. Drucker, Peter, op. cit., p. 190.
5. Anshen, Melvin, "The Management of Ideas," *Harvard Business Review*, July–August 1969, pp. 99–107.
6. Ibid., p. 101.
7. Ibid., p. 102.

Chapter 5
1. Burr, H. S. and Northrop, F. S. C., "The Electro Dynamic Theory of Life," *Main Currents in Modern Thought*, Vol. 19, No. 1, September 1962, p. 8. This notion of structure/process is as difficult to present as it is important. Burr and Northrop point to this structure/process unity. They say: "A unity of nature as a whole is impressed upon the compounding and aggregating of the microscopic particles to make complex nature one as well as many, a unity as well as an aggregate, a field which in part determines the behavior of each particle and process, as well as a complex continuum, in part constituted by the motion and interaction of the particle."
   see also Suares, Carlo, *The Cipher of Genesis* (London: Stuart & Watkins, 1970) for a review of ancient Hebrew as a structure/process language.
   see also Levi-Strauss, Claude, *Structural Anthropology* (London: Penguin University Books, 1963), p. 206, for the interaction of structure/process in the interpretation of myth.
2. This wisdom is called *prajna* in Sanskrit. Zen addresses itself directly to the emancipation and "cleansing" of *prajna* wisdom.
3. Stcherbatsky, Th., *Buddhist Logic*, Vol. I. (New York: Dover Publications, 1962), p. 119 et seq.

Chapter 6
1. Levinson, Harry, *The Exceptional Executive* (Cambridge: Harvard University Press, 1968), p. 34.
2. Jaques, Elliott, *Equitable Payment* (London: Heinemann, 1961), p. 71.
3. Koestler, Arthur, *The Act of Creation* (New York: Macmillan, 1964), p. 38.
4. ———, *The Ghost in the Machine* (London: Pan Books, 1967), p. 384. Ancient art was ruled by canons. Plato, referring to Egyptian artists, said, "If you inspect their paintings and reliefs on the spot, you will find that their work of ten thousand years ago—I mean the expression

not loosely, but quite literally—is neither better nor worse than that of today; the standard of art is identical in both cases." Plato, *Laws,* Book II. At one time in Egypt there were two sculptors who in separate towns worked on two parts of a statue. "When the two parts of the figure were brought together they fitted exactly, so that the statue appeared the work of one man." See Hambidge, Jay, *The Elements of Dynamic Symmetry* (New York: Dover Publications, 1919), p. xiv.

Chapter 7
1. Drucker, Peter, *The Age of Discontinuity* (New York: Harper & Row, 1969).
2. ———, "What We Can Learn from Japanese Management," *Harvard Business Review,* March–April 1971, pp. 11–22.

Chapter 8
1. Miller, J. G., "The Organization of Life," *Perspectives in Biology and Medicine,* Autumn 1965, pp. 107–25. It is worth pointing out that Miller saw a similar six-dimensional system to account for an organism. Other papers by Miller: "Living Systems—Cross Level Hypothesis," *Behavioral Science,* October 1965; "Living Systems—Structure and Process," *Behavioral Science,* October 1965.
2. Argyris, Chris, "Understanding and Increasing Organizational Effectiveness," *Commercial Letter of Canadian Imperial Bank of Commerce,* October 1968, p. 8.
3. ———, "How Tomorrow's Executives Will Make Decisions," *Think,* November–December 1967, p. 23.
4. Ferguson, C., "Coping with Organization Conflict," *Innovation,* No. 29, March 1972, pp. 36–43.
5. Argyris, Chris, "Understanding and Increasing Organizational Effectiveness," p. 2.
6. Kobayashi, Shigeru, *Creative Management* (New York: American Management Association, Inc., 1971).
7. Jaques, Elliott, "Preliminary Sketch of a General Structure of Executive Strata," *Glacier Project Papers* (London: Heinemann, 1965).

Chapter 9
1. White, K. K., *Understanding the Company Organization Chart* (New York: American Management Association, Inc., 1963), p. 24.
2. Koontz, H. and O'Donnell, C., *Principles of Management* (New York: McGraw-Hill, 1959), pp. 135–36.

3. Fisch, G. G., *Organization for Profit* (New York: McGraw-Hill, 1964), p. 48.
4. White, K. K., op. cit., pp. 37–38.
5. Ibid., p. 32.
6. Ibid., p. 33.
7. Ibid., loc. cit.
8. Bennett, J. G., *Dramatic Universe*, Vol. III, p. 18.
9. White, K. K., op. cit., p. 35.
10. Ibid., p. 33.
11. Ibid., loc. cit.
12. Klotz, Ambrose, "Line and Staff Today," *Administrative Management*, March 1968, pp. 20–21.
13. Dalton, Melville, "Conflicts Between Staff and Line Managerial Officers," *American Sociological Review*, 15, 1950, p. 343.
14. Ibid., p. 344.

Chapter 10
1. Drucker, Peter, *The Age of Discontinuity*, p. 96.

Chapter 11
1. Carpenter, Edmund, "Image Making in Arctic Art" in *Sign, Image and Symbol* (New York: Braziller, 1966), p. 208.

Chapter 12
1. Dale, E., op. cit.
2. Nelson, J. R. and Stevenson, H. W., *Profit in the Modern Economy* (Minneapolis, Minn.: University of Minnesota Press, 1967), p. 3.
3. Kozybski, Alfred, *Science and Sanity* (Lancaster, Pa.: Science Press, 1941), p. 110.
4. Galbraith, J. K., op. cit., p. 115.

Chapter 13
1. Jaques, Elliott, see for example, "Psycho-Analysis and the Current Economic Crisis" in *Work, Creativity, and Social Justice* (London: Heinemann, 1970).
2. Levinson, Harry, *The Exceptional Executive*.
3. Fromm, Erich, *Zen and Psychoanalysis* (London: George Allen & Unwin, 1960), p. 139.
4. Freud, Sigmund, *The Ego and the Id*, tr., J. Riviere (London: Hogarth Press, 1949), p. 27.
5. Ibid., p. 30.
6. Ibid., p. 40.
7. Ibid., p. 50.
8. Ibid., p. 56.

9. Ibid., loc. cit.
10. It would seem that there has been an awareness of the center-periphery polarity since very early times. Ancient monuments such as the pyramids, Stonehenge, and others were built within an area known as the *"vesica pisces."* This area is formed from two overlapping circles, *the center of one being on the periphery of the other.* This same symbol of two overlapping circles helps to explain the enigmatic account of creation given in Plato's *Timaeus.* This account was, according to Plato, derived from Atlantis. See *City of Revelation* by John Michell (London: Garnstone Press, 1972).

   See also *View Over Atlantis* by John Michell (London: Garnstone Press), p. 134. "The Vesica lies beneath the foundation of every great temple, those of antiquity and of early Christianity." According to Plotinus "every point is both at the center and periphery of all that exists. (See J. G. Bennett's *Dramatic Universe*, Vol. II, p. 121.) An interesting example of the center-periphery is shown in "Do Dual Organizations Exist?" in *Structural Anthropology* by Claude Levi-Strauss.
11. Eliade, Mircea, *Images and Symbols,* tr., P. Mairet (London: Harvill Press, 1961), p. 55.
12. *Sobbe Sankhara Dukkha*—The first noble truth of Buddhism. "One of the most meaningful words of any language is *dukkha*. It consists only of a prefix and a suffix, with nothing in between—which alone tells us much. Yet it sums up the built-in contradiction that makes up and keeps going the whole everchanging yet interdependent cosmic flow. *Du*—Short for *dvi,* similar to Greek *duo* and *dys,* meaning two; thus, asunder—which is precisely what ails the world to its hurt. *Kha*—May denote either a substantive or an activity. *Dukkha*—Two-ness or split action, meaning du-al(ity) or divisive(ness); the inner contradiction of opposites forming all movement of matter and mind, which we sense as the wrench or hurt of something gone wrong; inner conflict, ailment, hurt. Above quoted from "A Layman Looks into Pali," LeRoy, A. Born, *Middle Way, Journal of the Buddhist Society,* Vol. XLVIII, No. 3, November 1963, p. 133.

   The reader who would like to follow up the importance of the above to Western thinking is referred to *What Is Called Thinking* by Martin Heidegger, in particular to pp. 208–28. "Participles take part in both the nominal and the verbal meaning. . . . Blossoming, that is something blossoming and the act of blossoming . . . 'being' means something in being, and the act of being. . . . When we say 'Being,' it means 'Being of beings.' When we say 'beings' it means 'beings in respect of being.' We are always speaking *within* the duality. . . . Beings and being are in different places."

13. The notion of the primary word is developed by Martin Buber in *I and Thou,* tr., R. G. Smith (Edinburgh: Clark, 1937). However, Buber suggested two primary words: "I-thou" and "I-it." These it would seem would be secondary to "I-am-I?"

14. Horney, Karen, *The Neurotic Personality of Our Time* (New York: Norton, 1937).

15. Mowat, Farley, *Never Cry Wolf* (Boston: Little, Brown, 1963), pp. 94–98.

16. Benoit, Hubert, *Let Go!* tr., A. W. Low (London: George Allen & Unwin, 1954), p. 216. The word "is made of two parts; it brings with it a formal kernel or center and a formless halo which surrounds this center."

17. Spengler, Oswald, *The Decline of the West* (London: George Allen & Unwin, 1932), p. 123.

18. Koestler, Arthur, *The Ghost in the Machine,* p. 46.

19. Heidegger, Martin, *Existence and Being* (Chicago: Gateway, 1949), p. 336.

Chapter 14

1. Ardrey, Robert, *The Territorial Imperative* (New York: Dell, 1966).

2. Sartre, Jean Paul, *Being and Nothingness,* tr., H. E. Barnes (London: Methuen, 1957), p. 228.

3. Ibid., p. 222.

4. Ibid., p. 255.

5. Lorenz, Konrad, *Man Meets Dog,* tr., M. K. Wilson (London: Penguin, 1964), p. 108.

6. Ardrey, Robert, op. cit., p. 3.

7. Ibid., p. 51.

8. Ibid., p. 87.

9. Ibid., p. 52.

10. Ibid., p. 170.

11. Ibid., loc. cit.

12. Ibid., p. 52.

13. Miller, J. G., "The Organization of Life," p. 119.

14. Brown, W. "What is Work?" *Glacier Project Papers* (London: Heinemann, 1965), p. 70.

15. Rice, A. K., "Individual Group and Inter-Group Processes" *Human Relations,* Vol. 22, No. 6, December 1969, pp. 565–84.

16. Ibid.

17. Jung, C. G., *Psychology and Religion, West and East* (London: Routledge & Kegan Paul, 1958), p. 15.
18. See a hilarious account of this in the *Double Helix* by James D. Watson (New York: Signet Books).
19. Montague, Ashley, *The Human Revolution* (New York: Bantam Books, 1965), p. 116.
20. Riesman, Paul, "The Eskimo's Discovery of Man's Place in the Universe," in *Sign, Image and Symbol* (New York: Braziller, 1966), p. 228.
21. Ibid.
22. Ibid.
23. Eliade, Mircea, *Images and Symbols,* pp. 445–46. See also notion of "centering" developed by T. de Chardin in the *Phenomenon of Man* (New York: Harper and Brothers, 1959).
24. Ardrey, Robert, op. cit., p. 48.
25. Lorenz, Konrad, *On Aggression,* tr., M. Latzke (London: Methuen, 1966), p. 36.
26. Jaques, Elliott, "Industry's Human Needs," *Management Today,* May 1970.
27. Kobayashi, Shigeru, op. cit.
28. Conference Board 1973, *Corporate Organization Structure,* see, e.g., pp. 51, 73.

Chapter 15
1. Walker, A. H. and Lorsche, J. W., "Organizational Choice: Product vs. Function," *Harvard Business Review,* November–December 1968, p. 130.
2. Ibid., p. 129.
3. Ibid., p. 130.
4. Ibid., loc. cit.
5. Seeman, Melvin, "The Urban Alienation," *Journal of Personality and Social Psychology,* Vol. 19, No. 2, April 1971, p. 143.
6. Jung, C. G., *Psychology and Alchemy,* tr., R. F. C. Hull (London: Routledge & Kegan Paul, 1953), p. 15.
7. See for example, *The King and the Corpse* by Heinrich Zimmer (New York: Bollingen, 1948); *Mysterium Conjunctionis* by C. G. Jung, translated by R. F. C. Hull (New York: Bollingen, 1963); *Psychology and Religion, West and East* by C. G. Jung, p. 175 on paradox; "The Urban Alienation" by Melvin Seeman, *Journal of Personality and Social Psychology,* Vol. 19, No. 2, April 1971: The social scientists are also faced with the dilemma "between keeping a professional craft that is worthy of the name, and at the same time making investigations that illuminate on a scale commensurate with this known history and likely

future. The [dilemma] poses dangers on both sides: the danger in preserving the craft is that the work deteriorates into a kind of alienation in itself bound by technical rules, limited in vision, devoid of personal involvement, and largely oriented to careers. The danger on the side of relevance is that this deteriorates, too—into a subtle anti-intellectualism that is impatient with anything but the immediate, or into a kind of self-indulgence that emphasizes stance over analysis so that what becomes crucial is one's identification as a realist, radical, humanist, or whatever."

8. Jung, C. G., *Psychology and Religion, West and East,* p. 221. Bridgman, P. W., *The Way Things Are* (New York: Viking Press, 1961), pp. 6–7. Even in such a straightforward subject as arithmetic, the dilemma again appears. Bridgman says, "To prove mathematics free from potential contradiction one must use principles outside mathematics and then to prove that these principles do not conceal contradictions, one must use new principles beyond them. . . . Godel's theorem states that it is impossible to prove that a logical system, at least as complicated as arithmetic, contains no concealed contradictions by using only theorems which are derivable within the system. . . . It is tempting to generalize Godel's theorem to read that whenever we have a system dealing with itself we may expect to encounter maladjustments and infelicities, if not downright paradox. The insight that we can never get away from ourselves presents us with a situation of this sort."

Chapter 16

1. Lamouche, André, *Le Principe de Simplicité dans les Mathématiques et dans les Sciences Physiques* (Paris: Gauthier Villars, 1958), p. 25.
2. Seeman, M., op. cit.
3. Watson, J. B., *Behaviorism* (Chicago: University of Chicago Press, 1930), p. 198.
4. Heidegger, Martin, *Being and Time,* tr., J. MacQuarrie and E. Robinson (New York: Harper & Row, 1962), p. 51.
5. Abercrombie, M. L. J., *The Anatomy of Judgement* (London: Hutchinson, 1969).
6. Katz, David, *Gestalt Psychology* (London: Methuen, 1951), p. 47.
7. Holiday, Ensor, *Altair Designs* (London: Longman Ltd., 1974).
8. Koestler, Arthur, *The Ghost in the Machine,* pp. 194–98: "Recoil in order to be able to leap that much better."
9. Abercrombie, M. L. J., op. cit.
10. Ibid.

11. Russell, Bertrand, *Wisdom of the West* (New York: Premier Books, 1964), p. 74.
12. Attneave, Fred, "Multistability in Perception," *Scientific American,* December 1971, p. 67.
13. Lamouche, André, *L'Homme dans l'Harmonie Universelle* (Paris: La Colombe, 1963), p. 9.
14. Heidegger, Martin, *What Is a Thing?* (Chicago: Henry Regnery Co., Gateway Edition, 1967). See pp. 24–31 for a discussion of the role of "this" in philosophy.
15. Koestler, Arthur, *The Act of Creation* (New York: Macmillan, 1964).
16. McLuhan, M. and Nevitt, B., *Take Today: The Executive as Dropout* (New York: Harcourt, 1972). "By embracing both horns of a dilemma paradox leads to discovery."

Chapter 17

1. Ouspensky, P. D., *The Psychology of Man's Possible Evolution* (London: Hodder and Stoughton, 1951), p. 15.
2. Kierkegaard, S. A., *Purity of Heart Is to Will One Thing* (New York: Harper and Brothers, 1938).
3. Gable, Frank, *The Third Force* (New York: Grossman, 1970), p. 52.
4. Horney, Karen, op. cit.
5. Argyris, Chris, "How Tomorrow's Executives Will Make Decisions," *Think,* November–December 1967, p. 18.
6. On the value of Zen in developing intuition see, "Intuition in Zen Buddhism" by Akihisa Kondo, *American Journal of Psychoanalysis,* 1952, pp. 10–14.
7. Hauscha, Rudolf, *Nutrition* (London: Stuart and Watkins). Hauscha, speaking of Goethe, said: "He actually perceived the plants' primal being and would not accept Schiller's suggestion that all he saw was 'a mere idea.' The cosmos is full of such ideas, endowed with real being and each last one is a thought of God," p. 27.
8. Spengler, Oswald, op. cit., p. 202.
9. Livingston, J. S., "Myth of the Well-Educated Manager," *Harvard Business Review,* January–February 1971, pp. 79–89.
10. Drucker, Peter, "Our Top-Heavy Corporations," interview in *Dun's Review,* April 1971, pp. 38–41.
11. Livingston, J. S., op. cit.
12. Jung, C. G., *Psychology and Religion, West and East,* p. 312.
13. Pascal, Blaise, *Pensées: Thoughts on Religion and Other Subjects,* tr., W. F. Trotter (New York: Washington Square Press), p. 176.
14. Spengler, Oswald, op. cit., pp. 104–5.

15. Ibid.
16. Selye, Hans, *The Stress of Life* (New York: McGraw-Hill, 1956), p. 66.
17. Ibid. This idea of adaptive energy is known in Japanese Zen as *joriki* power which is developed through Zazen. This idea of an "energy of organization" has been the subject of a considerable amount of research and speculation. See, for example: *The Fields of Life* by Harold Burr (New York: Ballantine Books, Inc.); *Beyond Telepathy* by Andrija Paharich (Garden City: Doubleday & Co., Inc., 1962); *The Secret of Life* by Georges Lahkovsky (Rustington, Eng.: Health Science Press); *Selected Writings— An Introduction to Orgonomy* by Wilhelm Reich (New York: Farrar Straus & Giroux); *The States of Human Consciousness* by C. Daly King (New York: Universe Books, 1963); *The Phenomenon of Man* by Teilhard de Chardin (Washington, D.C.: Occidental, 1968).

    On the value of Zen in developing stress tolerance see Jodi Lawrence's *Alpha Brain Waves;* R. K. Wallace and H. Benson, "The Physiology of Meditation," *Scientific American,* February 1972, pp. 85–90; Gerald Jonas, *Visceral Learning* (New York: Viking Press), pp. 99–130.
18. Churchman, C. W., *Challenge to Reason* (New York: McGraw-Hill, 1968).
19. *Business Week,* "The New Management Finally Takes Over," August 1969.
20. Selye, H., op. cit., p. 54.
21. Ibid., p. 297.
22. Russell, Bertrand, *Autobiography, Vol. I, 1972 to World War I* (New York: Grosset & Dunlap, 1968).
23. For the value of Zen in developing communication, see Lesh, T. V., "Zen Meditation and the Development of Empathy in Counselors," *Journal of Humanistic Psychology,* Vol. 10, No. 1, Spring 1970, pp. 39–83.
24. Rogers, Carl, *On Becoming a Person* (Boston: Houghton Mifflin, 1961).
25. Ibid.
26. Hall, E. T., *The Silent Language* (Garden City: Doubleday & Co., Inc., 1959) and *The Hidden Dimension* (Garden City: Doubleday & Co., Inc., 1969).
27. Hall, E. T., *Silent Language,* p. 9.

Chapter 18

1. The fact of metals having responses similar to plants and human beings was established by Sir Jagadis Bose in 1900. In the book *The Secret Life of Plants* by P. Tompkin and C. Bird (New York: Harper & Row, 1972), the authors

say: "To meet the physiologists on their ground, Bose meticulously adapted his experiments to an accepted 'electromotive variation' to which they were accustomed and again got similar curves of muscles and metals responding to the effects of fatigue as to stimulating, depressing, and poisoning drugs."

2. Levinson, H., op. cit., p. 292.
3. Koestler, Arthur, *The Ghost in the Machine*, p. 369.
4. Stryk, L. and Ikemoto, T., *Zen: Poems, Prayers, Sermons, Anecdotes, Interviews* (Garden City: Doubleday & Co., Inc., 1965), p. 7.
5. Koestler, Arthur, *The Ghost in the Machine*, p. 382.
6. Yasutani, H., *Eight Beliefs in Buddhism* (private publication, 1965).

Chapter 19

1. Fromm, E., Suzuki, D., and de Martino, R., *Zen Buddhism and Psychoanalysis* (London: George Allen & Unwin, 1960), p. 30. Suzuki is quoting Rinzai, one of the most famous of Zen Masters.
2. Ibid. The method of the Master "consists in putting one in a dilemma, out of which one must contrive to escape not through logic indeed but through a mind of high order," p. 120.
3. Benoit, Hubert, *The Supreme Doctrine* (London: Routledge & Kegan Paul, 1950). The last chapter of Benoit's book is devoted to a study of the place of humiliation in Zen training.
4. Riesman, Paul, in *Sign, Image and Symbol* (New York: Braziller, 1966), p. 228.
5. Cortois, Flora, *An Experience of Enlightenment*, Zen Center of Los Angeles.

Chapter 20

1. Yampolsky, P. B. (translator), *The Zen Master Hakuin* (New York: Columbia University Press, 1971), p. 34. The practicality of Zen is stressed by all Zen Masters and is for this reason particularly suited to North America. See also the introduction by Philip Kapleau to *Zen Keys* (Garden City: Doubleday & Co., Inc., 1974).
2. Tohei, Koichi, *Aikido in Daily Life* (Tokyo: Rikugei Publishing House, 1966). The author gives some simple demonstrations of the value of *hara*.
   see also Durckheim, Karlfried, *Hara* (London: George Allen & Unwin, 1962).
3. Kapleau, Philip, *Three Pillars of Zen* (New York, Harper & Row, 1966).

4. Ibid., p. 4.
5. Reps, Paul, *Zen Flesh, Zen Bones* (Tokyo: Charles E. Tuttle Co., 1957), p. 92.
6. Kapleau, Philip, *The Wheel of Death* (New York: Harper & Row, 1971).
7. Stryk, L. and Ikemoto, Takashi, op. cit., pp. 9 and 11.
8. Kapleau, Philip, *The Wheel of Death*, p. 67.
9. Ibid.
10. Ibid., p. 32.
11. Guenther, H. V., *The Life and Teaching of Naropa* (Oxford: Oxford University Press, 1963), p. 116.

BIBLIOGRAPHY

Anshen, Melvin, "The Management of Ideas," *Harvard Business Review*, July–August 1969, pp. 99–107.

Ardrey, Robert, *The Territorial Imperative* (New York: Dell, 1966).

Argyris, Chris, "How Tomorrow's Executives Will Make Decisions," *Think*, November–December 1967, pp. 18–23.

——, "Understanding and Increasing Organizational Effectiveness," *Commercial Letter of Canadian Imperial Bank of Commerce*, October 1968.

Attneave, Fred, "Multistability in Perception," *Scientific American*, December 1971, pp. 63–71.

Baker, Frank, "Review of General Systems Concepts and Their Relevance for Medical Care," *Systematics*, Vol. 7, No. 3, 1969, pp. 209, 299.

Bennett, J. G., *The Dramatic Universe*, Vols. I–IV (London: Hodder & Stoughton, 1956, 1961, 1967, 1966).

——, "General Systematics," *Systematics*, Vol. 1, No. 1, June 1963, pp. 5–18.

——, "Systematics and General Systems Theory," *Systematics*, Vol. 1, No. 2, September 1963, pp. 105–9.

——, "Systematics and Systems Theories," *Systematics*, Vol. 7, No. 4, March 1970, pp. 273–78.

——, "Sufi Spiritual Techniques," *Systematics*, Vol. 7, No. 3, December 1969, pp. 244–60.

Benoit, Hubert, *The Supreme Doctrine* (London: Routledge & Kegan Paul, 1950).

——, *Let Go!* tr. A. W. Low (London: George Allen & Unwin, 1962).

Benson, H. and Wallace, R. K., "The Physiology of Meditation," *Scientific American*, February 1972, pp. 85–90.

Berkwitt, George J., "Those Disappearing Executives," *Surplus Record*, August 1972, pp. 26–31.

Bernal, J. D., *The Origin of Life* (London: Weidenfeld & Nicholson, 1969).

Bertalanffy, Ludwig von, *General System Theory* (New York: George Braziller, 1968).

Blum, M. L., *Industrial Psychology: Its Theoretical and Social Foundations* (New York: Harper & Row, 1968).

Blyth, R. H., *Zen and Zen Classics, Vol. 4* (Tokyo: Hokuseido Press, 1966).

Born, Leroy A., "A Layman Looks into Pali," *Middle Way*, Vol. XLVIII, No. 3.

Boulding, K. E., "General Systems Theory—The Skeleton of Science," *General Systems Yearbook*, No. 1, 1956, pp. 11–17.

Bridgman, P. W., *The Way Things Are* (New York: Viking, 1961).

Brown, E. C., Erwin, T. J., and Putney, R. T., "Zazen and Biofeedback Training in the Autocontrol of the Alpha Rhythm of the Brain," Georgia State University, Research Paper (unpublished).

Brown, Wilfred, *Explorations in Management* (London: Heinemann, 1960).

———, "Organization and Science," *Glacier Project Papers* (London: Heinemann, 1965).

———, "What is Work?" *Glacier Project Papers* (London: Heinemann, 1965).

Buber, Martin, *I and Thou*, tr., R. G. Smith (Edinburgh: Clark, 1937).

Burr, H. S. and Northrop, F. S. C., "The Electro Dynamic Theory of Life," *Main Currents in Modern Thought*, Vol. 19, No. 1, September 1962, p. 8.

Business Week, "The New Management Finally Takes Over," August 23, 1969.

Carpenter, Edmund, "Image Making in Arctic Art," *Sign, Image and Symbol* (New York: Braziller, 1966).

Chang, Garma, C. C., *The Buddhist Teaching of Totality* (University Park, Pa.: Pennsylvania State University Press, 1971).

Conference Board, *Corporate Organization Structure.*

Courtois, Flora, *An Experience of Enlightenment*, Zen Center of Los Angeles.

Dale, Ernest, *Organization* (New York: American Management Association, Inc., 1970).

Dalton, Melville, "Conflicts Between Staff and Line Managerial Officers," *American Sociological Review*, 15, 1950, pp. 342–51.

DeMaria, A. et al., *Manager Unions?* (New York: American Management Association, Inc., 1972).

Drucker, Peter, *Landmarks of Tomorrow* (New York: Harper Colophon Books, 1957).

———, *The Age of Discontinuity* (New York: Harper & Row, 1969).

———, "Our Top-Heavy Corporations," interview in *Dun's Review*, April 1971, pp. 38–41.

Durkheim, Karlfried, *Hara* (London: George Allen & Unwin, 1962).

Eliade, Mircea, *Images and Symbols*, tr., P. Mairet (London: Harvill Press, 1961).

Erwin, T. J., Brown, E. C., and Putney, R. T., "Zazen and Biofeedback Training in the Autocontrol of the Alpha Rhythm of the Brain," Georgia State University, Research Paper (unpublished).

Fange, E. K. von, *Professional Creativity* (New York: Prentice-Hall, 1959).

Fausch, David A., *Business Week*, September 25, 1971.

Ferguson, C., "Coping with Organizational Conflict," *Innovation*, No. 29, March 1972, pp. 36–43.

Fisch, G. G., *Organization for Profit* (New York: McGraw-Hill, 1964).

Freud, Sigmund, *The Ego and the Id*, tr., J. Riviere (London: Hogarth Press, 1949).

Fromm, Erich, *The Revolution of Hope* (New York: Harper & Row, 1968).

Fromm, Erich, Suzuki, D. T., and de Martino, Richard, *Zen Buddhism and Psychoanalysis* (London: George Allen & Unwin, 1960).

Galbraith, J. K., *The New Industrial State* (Boston: Houghton Mifflin, 1967).

Gautama Buddha, *The Dhammapada*, tr., Irving Babbitt (New York: New Directions, 1965).

Greiner, Larry E., "Patterns of Organization Change," *Harvard Business Review*, May–June 1967, pp. 119–30.

Guenther, H. V., *The Life and Teaching of Naropa* (Oxford: Oxford University Press, 1963).

Hall, Edward T., *The Silent Language* (Garden City: Doubleday & Co., Inc., 1959).

——, *The Hidden Dimension* (Garden City: Doubleday & Co., Inc., 1969).

Hambidge, Jay, *The Elements of Dynamic Symmetry*, Yale, 1919, Dover Publications.

Hanh, Thichnhat, *Zen Keys*, tr., Jean and Albert Low (Garden City: Doubleday & Co., Inc., 1974).

Hauscha, Rudolf, *Nutrition* (London: Stuart and Watkins).

Heidegger, Martin, *Existence and Being* (Chicago: Gateway, 1949).

——, *Being and Time*, tr., J. MacQuarrie and E. Robinson (New York: Harper & Row, 1962).

——, *Discourse on Thinking*, tr., John M. Anderson and E. H. Freund (New York: Harper Torch Books, 1966).

——, *What Is a Thing?* tr., W. B. Barton Jr. and V. Deutsch (Chicago: Henry Regnery Co., 1967).

——, *What Is Called Thinking*, tr., F. Wieck and J. G. Gray (New York: Harper Torch Books, 1972).

Herrick, Neal Q. and Sheppard, Harold L., *Where Have All the Robots Gone?* (New York: The Free Press, 1972).

Herzberg, Frederick, *Work and the Nature of Man* (New York: World Publishing, 1966).

Hodgson, A. M., "The Solution of Technical Problems by Groups," #1—*Systematics*, Vol. 2, No. 1, June 1964, pp. 1–46. #2—*Systematics*, Vol. 2, No. 3, December 1964, pp. 177–213. #3—*Systematics*, Vol. 2, No. 4, March 1965, pp. 298–322.

Holiday, Ensor, *Altair Designs* (London: Longman Ltd., 1974).

Horney, Karen, *The Neurotic Personality of Our Time* (New York: Norton, 1937).

Husserl, Edmund, *Ideas—A General Introduction to Pure Phenomenology* (London: George Allen & Unwin, 1931).

Ikemoto, Takashi and Stryk, Lucien, *Zen: Poems, Prayers, Sermons, Anecdotes, Interviews* (Garden City: Doubleday & Co., Inc., 1965).

Irwin, James B., *To Rule the Night* (New York: Ballantine Books, 1963).

Jaques, Elliott, *Equitable Payment* (London: Heinemann, 1961).

——, *Work, Creativity, and Social Justice* (London: Heinemann, 1970).

——, "Preliminary Sketch of a General Structure of Executive Strata," *Glacier Project Papers* (London: Heinemann, 1965).

Johnson, R. A., Kast, F. E., and Rosenzweig, J. E., *Theory and Management of Systems* (New York: McGraw-Hill, 1963).

Jonas, Gerald, *Visceral Learning* (New York: Viking Press, 1973).

Jung, C. G., *Mysterium Conjunctionis*, tr., R. F. C. Hull (New York: Bollingen, 1963).

——, "On Psychic Energy," *The Structure and Dynamics of the Psyche*, tr., R. F. C. Hull (London: Routledge & Kegan Paul, 1960).

——, *Psychology and Alchemy*, tr., R. F. C. Hull (London: (Routledge & Kegan Paul, 1953).

——, *Symbols of Transformation*, tr., R. F. C. Hull (New York: Bollingen, 1956).

——, "Psychological Approach to the Dogma of the Trinity," *Psychology and Religion, West and East*, tr., R. F. C. Hull (London: Routledge & Kegan Paul, 1958).

——, "Transformation Symbolism of the Mass," *Psychology and Religion, West and East*, tr., R. F. C. Hull (London: Routledge & Kegan Paul, 1958).

Kapleau, Philip, *The Three Pillars of Zen* (New York: Harper & Row, 1966).

——, *The Wheel of Death* (New York: Harper & Row, 1971).

Katz, David, *Gestalt Psychology* (London: Methuen, 1951).

Kast, F. E., Johnson, R. A. and Rosenzweig, J. E., *Theory and Management of Systems* (New York: McGraw-Hill, 1963).

Kepes, Gyorgy, ed., *Sign, Image and Symbol* (New York: Braziller, 1966).

Kierkegaard, Soren, *Purity of Heart Is to Will One Thing*, tr., D. Steere (New York: Harper and Brothers, 1938).

Klotz, Ambrose, "Line and Staff Today," *Administrative Management*, March 1968, pp. 20–22.

Kobayashi, Shigeru, *Creative Management* (New York: American Management Association, Inc., 1971).

Koestler, Arthur, *The Act of Creation* (New York: Macmillan, 1964).

——, *The Ghost in the Machine* (London: Pan Books, 1967).

Kondo, A., "Intuition in Zen Buddhism," *American Journal of Psychoanalysis*, 1952, pp. 10–14.

——, "Zen in Psychotherapy, the Virtue of Sitting," *Chicago Review*, Vol. 12, No. 2, 1958, pp. 57–64.

Koontz, H. and O'Donnell, C., *Principles of Management* (New York: McGraw-Hill, 1959).

Korzybski, Alfred, *Science and Sanity* (Lancaster, Pa.: Science Press, 1941).

Lamouche, André, *L'Homme dans l'Harmonie Universelle* (Paris: La Colombe, 1963).

——, *Le Principe de Simplicité dans les Mathématiques et dans les Sciences Physiques* (Paris: Gauthier Villars, 1958).

Lawrence, Jodi, *Alpha Brain Wave* (New York: Avon, 1973).

Lesh, T. V., "Zen Meditation and the Development of Empathy in Counselors," *Journal of Humanistic Psychology*, Vol. 10, No. 1, Spring 1970, pp. 39–83.

Levi-Strauss, Claude, *Structural Anthropology* (London: Penguin University Books, 1963).

Levinson, Harry, *The Exceptional Executive* (Cambridge: Harvard University Press, 1968).

Levitt, Theodore, "Marketing Myopia," *Harvard Business Review*, July–August 1960.

Lewin, Kurt, *Field Theory in Social Science* (New York: Harper & Row, 1951).

Livingston, J. S., "Myth of the Well-Educated Manager," *Harvard Business Review*, January–February 1971, pp. 79–89.

Lorenz, Konrad, *Man Meets Dog*, tr., M. K. Wilson (London: Penguin Books, 1964).

Lorsche, J. W. and Walker, A. H., "Organizational Choice: Product vs. Function," *Harvard Business Review*, November–December 1968, pp. 129–38.

——, *On Aggression*, tr., M. Latzke (London: Methuen, 1966).

Low, A. W., "The Systematics of a Business Organization," *Systematics*, Vol. 4, No. 3, December 1966, pp. 248–79.

McFeely, Wilbur M., *Organization Change—Perceptions and Realities*, New York Conference Board, 1972.

McGloughlin, J. Brian, *Urban and Regional Planning* (London: Faber & Faber, 1969).

McGregor, Douglas, *The Human Side of Enterprise* (New York: McGraw-Hill, 1960).

McLuhan, M. and Nevitt, B., *Take Today: The Executive as Dropout* (New York: Harcourt, 1972).

McQuaig, J. H., "What to Look for When You're Hiring," *Supervisory Management*, Vol. 17, No. 1, January 1972, pp. 17–23.

Mace, Myles L., *Directors: Myth and Reality* (Boston: Harvard Business School, Division of Research, 1971).

Martz, Louis L., *The Poetry of Meditation* (New Haven: Yale, 1954).

Maslow, Abraham, *Towards a Psychology of Being* (New York: Van Nostrand, 1962).

Masunaga, Reiho, *The Soto Approach to Zen* (Tokyo: Buddhist Society Press, 1958).

Matthews, P. T., *The Explosion of Science: The Assault on the Atom* (New York: Meredith Press, 1967).

Meadows, D., et al., *The Limits to Growth* (Washington, D.C.: Potomac Associates Books, 1972).

Michell, John, *City of Revelation* (London: Garnstone Press, 1972).

——, *View Over Atlantis* (London: Garnstone Press, 1969).

Miller, E. J., "Technology, Territory and Time: The Internal Differentiation of Complex Systems," *Human Relations*, No. 12, 1959, pp. 243–72.

Miller, J. G., "The Organization of Life," *Perspectives in Biology and Medicine*, Autumn 1965, pp. 102–25.

——, "Living Systems—Structure and Process," *Behavioral Science*, October 1965.

——, "Living Systems—Cross Level Hypotheses," *Behavioral Science*, October 1965.

Montague, Ashley, *The Human Revolution* (New York: Bantam Books, 1965).

Mowat, Farley, *Never Cry Wolf* (Boston: Little Brown, 1963).

Myers, M. Scott, "Who Are Your Motivated Workers," *Harvard Business Review*, January–February 1964.

Nelson, J. R. and Stevenson, H. W., *Profit in the Modern Economy* (Minneapolis, Minn.: University of Minnesota Press, 1967).

Nevitt, B. and McLuhan, M., *Take Today: The Executive as Dropout* (New York: Harcourt, 1972).

Northrop, F. S. C. and Burr, H. S., "The Electro Dynamic Theory of Life," *Main Currents in Modern Thought,* Vol. 19, No. 1, September 1962, p. 8.

O'Donnell, C. and Koontz, H., *Principles of Management* (New York: McGraw-Hill, 1959).

Ouspensky, P. D., *The Psychology of Man's Possible Evolution* (London: Hodder and Stoughton, 1951).

Pascal, Blaise, *Pensées: Thoughts on Religion and Other Subjects,* tr., W. F. Trotter (New York: Washington Square Press, 1965).

Putney, R. T., Brown, E. C. and Erwin, T. J., "Zazen and Biofeedback Training in the Autocontrol of the Alpha Rhythm of the Brain," Georgia State University, Research Paper (unpublished).

Reich, Wilhelm, *Selected Writings: An Introduction to Orgonomy* (New York: Noonday Press, 1961).

Reps, Paul, *Zen Flesh, Zen Bones* (Tokyo: Charles E. Tuttle, 1957).

Rice, A. K., *The Enterprise and Its Environment* (London: Tavistock Publications, 1963).

——, "Individual, Group and Inter-Group Processes," *Human Relations,* Vol. 22, No. 6, December 1969, pp. 565–84.

Riesman, Paul, "The Eskimo's Discovery of Man's Place in the Universe," *Sign, Image and Symbol* (New York: Braziller, 1966).

Rogers, Carl R., *On Becoming a Person* (Boston: Houghton Mifflin, 1961).

Rosenzweig, J. E., Johnson, R. A. and Kast, F. E., *Theory and Management of Systems* (New York: McGraw-Hill, 1963).

Russell, Bertrand, *Autobiography, Vol. I, 1972 to World War I* (New York: Grosset & Dunlap, 1968).

——, "Scientific Method in Philosophy," *Our Knowledge of the External World* (London: George Allen & Unwin, 1914).

——, *Wisdom of the West* (New York: Premier Books, 1964).

Samaras, T. T., "Baseline Management," *Supervisory Management,* Vol. 16, No. 12, December 1971, pp. 7–12.

Sartre, Jean Paul, *Being and Nothingness,* tr., H. E. Barnes (London: Methuen, 1957).

Schumacher, E. F., *Small Is Beautiful* (New York: Harper & Row, 1973).

Seeman, Melvin, "The Urban Alienation," *Journal of Personality and Social Psychology,* Vol. 19, No. 2, April 1971.

248

Selye, Hans, *The Stress of Life* (New York: McGraw-Hill, 1956).

Sharp, F. R., "Lessons from Armed Forces Unification," *University of Western Ontario Quarterly*, Spring 1968, pp. 7–19.

Shaw, M. E., "Scaling Group Tasks: A Method for Dimensional Analysis," University of Florida, Technical Report No. 1, July 1963.

Sheppard, Harold L., and Herrick, Neal Q., *Where Have All the Robots Gone?* (New York: The Free Press, 1972).

Sluckin, W., *Minds and Machines* (London: Penguin Books, Ltd., 1954).

Spengler, Oswald, *The Decline of the West* (London: George Allen & Unwin, 1932).

Stcherbatsky, Th., *Buddhist Logic*, Vol. 1 (New York: Dover Publications, 1962).

Stryk, Lucien and Ikemoto, Takashi, *Zen: Poems, Prayers, Sermons, Anecdotes, Interviews* (Garden City: Doubleday & Co., Inc., 1965).

Suares, Carlo, *The Cipher of Genesis* (London: Stuart & Watkins, 1970).

Suzuki, D. T., Fromm, Erich, and Martino, Richard de, *Zen Buddhism and Psychoanalysis* (London: George Allen & Unwin, 1960).

Suzuki, Shunryu, *Zen Mind, Beginner's Mind* (Tokyo: Weatherhill, 1970).

Tarnowieski, D., *The Changing Success Ethic* (New York: American Management Association, Inc., 1973).

Tawney, R. H., *Religion and the Rise of Capitalism* (New York: Mentor, 1954).

Thompson, James D., *Organizations in Action* (New York: McGraw-Hill, 1967).

Tilles, Seymour, "How to Evaluate Corporate Strategy," *Harvard Business Review*, July–August 1963, pp. 111–21.

Tohei, Koichi, *Aikido in Daily Life* (Tokyo: Rikugei Publishing House, 1966).

Trist, E. L., et al., *Organizational Choice* (London: Tavistock, 1963).

Unamuno, Miguel de, *The Tragic Sense of Life* (London: Fontana, 1921).

Walker, A. H. and Lorsche, J. W., "Organizational Choice: Product vs. Function," *Harvard Business Review*, November–December 1968, pp. 129–38.

Wallace, R. K. and Benson, H., "The Physiology of Meditation," *Scientific American*, February 1972, pp. 85–90.

Watson, J. B., *Behaviorism* (Chicago: University of Chicago Press, 1930).

——, *Double Helix* (New York: Signet Books, 1968).

White, K. K., *Understanding the Company Organization Chart* (New York: American Management Association, Inc., 1963).

Yampolsky, P. B. (translator), *The Zen Master Hakuin* (New York: Columbia University Press, 1971).

Yasutani, H., *Eight Beliefs of Buddhism* (Private Publication, 1965).

Zimmer, Heinrich, *Myths and Symbols in Indian Art and Civilization* (New York: Harper & Row, 1962).

——, *The King and the Corpse* (New York: Meridian, 1960).

INDEX